Personal Training in Europe

The most comprehensive international study on Personal Training

Colophon

Copyrights
BlackBoxPublishers
EuropeActive

Editors/Authors
Niels Gronau and Gregor Titze;
edelhelfer GmbH, EuropeActive

Grammar
Cliff Collins

A publication of
EuropeActive, Brussels, Belgium &
BlackBoxPublishers, Den Bosch, the Netherlands.

Design
Hilly Goedhart, Fitbrand

Please order via http://www.europeactive.eu

ISBN/EAN
9789082787917

© **Copyright 2018**

All rights reserved. Nothing in this publication may be multiplied, stored in an automated data file, or made public, in any form, whether electronic, mechanical, by means of photo copies or in any other way, without prior written consent from EuropeActive and BlackBoxPublishers (RedBox BV).

Table of content

Preface EuropeActive		6
Preface Project Team		8
1.	Introduction to Personal Training: A snap shot of recent studies By Jan Middelkamp and Peter Wolfhagen	12
2	Personal Training Market Insights: An exploratory survey amongst European Personal Trainers By Niels Gronau and Gregor Titze	48
3	National Data Compilation	138
4	Perspectives on the Personal Training Market	170
5	Method	220
About EuropeActive, edelhelfer, Start2Move and BlackBoxPublishers		224

Preface EuropeActive

Dear reader,

The people element is crucial for any business. Many fitness operators are focussed on their Personal Trainers. The motivations of staff in the fitness sector and other defining characteristics, however, always remained unknown. With people as crucial element of the business, what motivates Personal Trainers to work in the health and fitness sector? And what are other defining characteristics of this group?

For the first time, total numbers of Personal Trainers per country and other defining characteristics such as employment status, prices charged, training offering and supplementary services are bundled in a single study on Personal Trainers.

Authored by renowned market research experts, Personal Training in Europe provides this insight as well as insights into the Personal Trainers customers; what type of customers can be identified and what do customers expect from Personal Trainers.

For EuropeActive, personal training is an important and growing segment of the health and fitness industry. This book Personal Training in Europe adds detailed and reliable knowledge and understanding of this growing market segment, and therefore would like to express my gratitude to the authors for making this important step forward.

The more we understand the people element of the fitness sector, the better the chances are to fulfil EuropeActive's mission to get more people, more active, more often.

Happy reading!

Nathalie Smeeman
Executive Director
EuropeActive

About EuropeActive
EuropeActive is the European Association that provides the unique voice for the fitness, physical activity, and wellbeing sector at the EU level in Brussels.

Preface Project Team

Dear Reader,

In front of you lies a unique document which is the first of its kind. It is the most comprehensive international research available to date on Personal Training. Based our history of research projects in the health and fitness market, EuropeActive and edelhelfer teamed up to improve the availability of reliable and sound data on this exciting market segment.

With the support from our partners miha bodytec as well as TomTom and in cooperation with BlackBoxPublishers we are able to present a report with data on the European Personal Training market in the most detailed way and for the first time. The report is based on extensive desk research, interviews with renowned industry experts but in particular an in-depth online questionnaire, that was answered by more than 3,000 Personal Trainers in Europe.

First of all, we would like to thank all Personal Trainers that shared their personal data as well as their view on the market with us. We also want to thank the individual national institutions that helped to address and motivate their contacts to participate in our research. Without the support of all of them it would not be possible to complete an analysis like this.

In addition to the results of our research project we are happy to have an introductory snap shot on recent studies on Personal Training written by Jan Middelkamp and Peter Wolfhagen. In addition, we have a group of prominent interview partners that give us their view on Personal Training from different perspectives of the industry and, thereby, complement our analysis of this exciting segment.

We hope our work arouses your interest and will be valuable for your business. In any case, we would be grateful to receive your feedback and contribution for upcoming surveys. It is only with the collaboration of all market participants that the necessary quality of information for the future development of our industry can be realised.

Have a joyful read!

Julian Berriman
EuropeActive

Niels Gronau
edelhelfer

1

Introduction to Personal Training: A snap shot of recent studies

1. Introduction to Personal Training: A snap shot of recent studies

Jan Middelkamp
Dr. Jan Middelkamp (PhD) is a fitness entrepreneur, researcher in health behaviour change and a previous COO of multiple international fitness chains. Visit: www.janmiddelkamp.com.

Peter Wolfhagen
Drs Peter Wolfhagen (MSc) is an exercise scientist, consultant and international presenter on member retention and behaviour change.

1.1 Introduction

In Europe, as in the rest of the world, Personal Training is on the move and developing rapidly. On Personal Training, there are plenty opinions, personal publications, etcetera. It is like football; the whole nation is an expert. But what is known about this profession from independent (scientific) research and which lessons can be learned from studies on Personal Training around the globe? In this chapter, an introduction to Personal Training is presented based on research, discussing topics such as profiles, activities, and success factors of Personal Trainers, plus profiles of Personal Training customers.

1.2 Personal Training defined

What is Personal Training? Ask this question to a group of professionals and discussions will explode. Personal Training is a generic name for a palette of activities and is defined in multiple ways. It could be called a container term, because almost everything fits inside. The broad character of Personal Training has advantages, disadvantages, beauties and flaws. The pluralism of this term and this discipline offers room to various angles and shapes. However, this versatility also creates obscurities, confusion and can lead to disappointments for customers. Organizations like ACSM provide definitions on Personal Training and Personal Trainer. In Table 1.1 some ad random selected definitions of a Personal Trainer are summarised.

The definitions or descriptions in Table 1.1 mainly describe what the profession of a Personal Trainer should encompass according to the organisation. As always, all definitions are discussable and have pros and cons. For example, the fact that a Personal Trainer does not explicitly have to perform a paid activity (fee-based) is notable. In Europe, Personal Training is still a relatively new phenomenon for the fitness sector in general and towards consumers.

What should a consumer expect of a Personal Trainer? And when is a person qualified to use the label "Personal Trainer"? There is, and perhaps will never be a dominant and global definition of a Personal Trainer or Personal Training. Of course, this is key to define for example the Personal Training market, but cohesion on this topic is limited. In this chapter, an umbrella approach of Personal Training will be used, meaning that Personal Training is defined in different ways, depending on the actual study presented.

Until now, the professional title Personal Trainer is not protected in most countries, so anyone can call themselves a Personal Trainer. This process is still in its infancy in Europe, but also in other continents, which is partly due to the broad interpretation given to the profession of Personal Training. EuropeActive (2011) took important steps with the development of standards to more explicitly define this profession (at level 4 within the European Qualification Framework; EQF). And differentiate it from other professions such as fitness instructors (EQF level 3). The standards are an important step but implementing them into the fitness sector and communicating it to a broader public is a long-term process which just has started.

Organisation	Definition or description
NSCA (2004)	A Personal Trainer is a fitness professional involved in exercise prescription and instruction. They motivate clients by setting goals and providing feedback and accountability to clients. Personal Trainers also measure their client's strengths and weaknesses with fitness assessments. These fitness assessments may also be performed before and after an exercise program to measure their client's improvements in physical fitness. They may also educate their clients in many other aspects of wellness besides exercise, including general health and nutrition guidelines. Qualified Personal Trainers recognise their own areas of expertise. If a Personal Trainer suspects that one of his or her clients has a medical condition that could prevent the client from safe participation in an exercise program, they must refer the client to the proper health professional for prior clearance.
ACSM (2007)	The ACSM certified Personal Trainer is a fitness professional involved in developing and implementing an individualised approach to exercise leadership in healthy populations and/or those individuals with medical clearance to exercise. Using a variety of teaching techniques, the trainer is proficient in leading and demonstrating safe and effective methods of exercise by applying the fundamental principles of exercise science. The ACSM certified Personal Trainer is proficient in writing appropriate exercise recommendations, leading and demonstrating safe and effective methods of exercise, and motivating individuals to begin and to continue with their healthy behaviours.
EuropeActive (2011)	A Personal Trainer's role includes designing, implementing and valuating exercise/physical activity programmes for a range of individual clients by collecting and analysing client information to ensure the effectiveness of personal exercise programmes. A Personal Trainer should also actively encourage potential clients/members to participate in and adhere to regular exercise/physical activity programmes, employing appropriate motivational strategies to achieve this.

Table 1.1: Definitions or descriptions of a Personal Trainer.

1.3 Personal Training development

Around the globe, Personal Training markets show different levels of development. In general, the United States of America are perceived as a fundamental market for Personal Training. Many point to the

Jack Lalanne Show in 1951, as inspiring the development of Personal Training in the US. According to Tharratt and Rutgers (2016), the first celebrity Personal Trainer, during the 1880s, was Louis Durlacher of Germany, also known as Professor Attila. He travelled the world performing feats of balance and strength. During his travels, attendees, many of whom were dignitaries, asked Attila for exercise advice. Consequently, he found himself the trainer of dignitaries, including luminaries such as Alexander III, Czar of Russia, King George of Greece, King Edward VII of England, Cornelius Vanderbilt and Baron Rothschild of France. In 1886 he opened what is possibly the first Personal Training studio in London, England. In 1894, nearly a decade after opening his studio in London, he moved to New York and opened Attila's Studio and School of Physical Culture. Professor Attila is also attributed with being a pioneer of sport specific training, as well as Personal Training for women.

There is limited information available on the historical development of Personal Training around the globe. Below, some markets will be discussed briefly.

North America
In the United States, 261,100 registered fitness trainers and aerobics instructors were counted in 2008. Approximately 149,000 were (also) Personal Trainers (US Bureau of Labor Statistics, 2010). Personal Training in Canada has shown substantial developments as well. For example, Goodlife, a fitness chain of over 300 clubs, employs approx. 2,000 fulltime Personal Trainers.

United Kingdom
In Europe, the most developed Personal Training market appears to be the United Kingdom. IBISWorld (2017) provides the Personal Trainers market research report with key analysis and statistics of this sector. They describe the UK Personal Training sector as highly fragmented and populated by owner-operators. The report states that: "Typically, Personal Trainers begin their career path by working in a gym after they obtain their qualifications, as gyms provide clients and high-quality machinery that independent trainers may not be able to access. Personal Trainers working at gyms are required to pay operation fees to their host venues. This is usually paid either as a percentage from each session or as a flat monthly rental fee. As they progress in their careers, the majority of Personal Trainers prefer to turn independent in order to maximise their salary." According to the 2017 report, the sector is expected to

perform well with revenue forecast to rise at compound annual rate of 2.9% over the period, to total £635m.

The Netherlands
Recently, multiple market studies were conducted on Personal Training in The Netherlands (Middelkamp, Wolfhagen and Wouters, 2017). It appears difficult to conclude the overall number of Personal Trainers in this small country, but a clear picture was taken from the top 11 chains (like Basic-Fit, FitForFree and Fitland). On average, a chain in The Netherlands has two Personal Trainers per club, with the lowest at Anytime (0.44) and Optisport (0.5). The highest number of trainers per club are at HealthCity (8.43). Basic-Fit, the European market leader in number of clubs (500+ end of 2017) has on average 1.53 trainer per club. In total, 1099 Personal Trainers work at the top 11 chains (double counts are possible), mostly within a rent model. In 2017, there are 623 Personal Training studios in The Netherlands. See more details in paragraph 1.8.

1.4 Profiles of Personal Trainers

More information is available on profiles of Personal Trainers. A clear profile emerged from research by Horn (2011) on Personal Training in Germany. This survey was sent out to 2,805 trainers with a response of 244, so a response rate of approximately 9%. For instance, the Personal Trainers from this study appear to have an average age of 36 years old, with a variation of 22 to 59 years. Personal Trainers in Germany are mostly men (60%), are highly educated, often in exercise science. The study by Horn also showed that the proportion of Personal Trainer that practice their trade fulltime versus parttime is changing. In 2004, this was 55% versus 45%, in 2011, 66% worked fulltime and only 34% parttime. 13% work as part of a team in a fitness club. In Germany, fulltime Personal Trainers earn 3.200 EUR net a month on average.

In a more recent study, Titze and Gronau (2015) of edelhelfer surveyed 225 German trainers and reported close to Horn that 66% of the trainers are male, with 38.7 as an average age. 74% expressed that Personal Training was their main profession and 86% operates as an independent contractor. One third of the German trainers was active less than five years. In terms of education, the largest group reported to be educated at level three of the European Qualification Framework (EQF). See Figure 1.1.

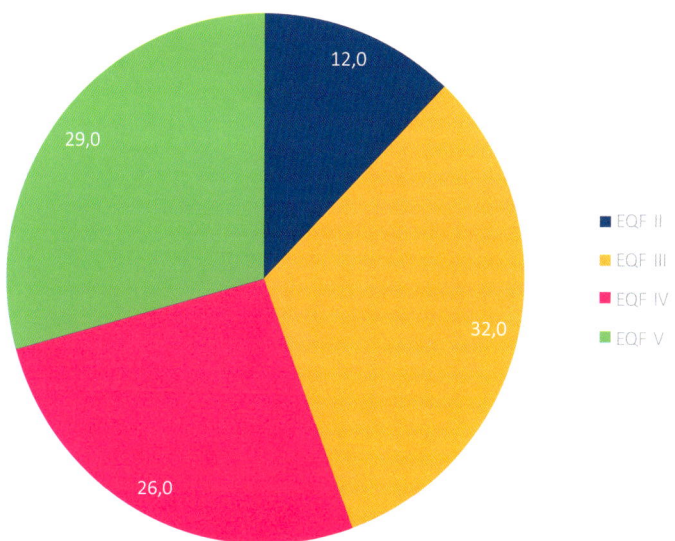

Figure 1.1: Educational levels of Personal Trainers in Germany based on self-report.

A recently conducted survey study with a response of 207 Personal Trainers in The Netherlands (Middelkamp, Wolfhagen and Wouters, 2017) demonstrated that most trainers are young in their profession and are active for less than three years (see Figure 1.2). Of this group, 23% are working in an employee model and 21% in a rent model. A substantial group operates their own Personal Training studio (approx. 30%).

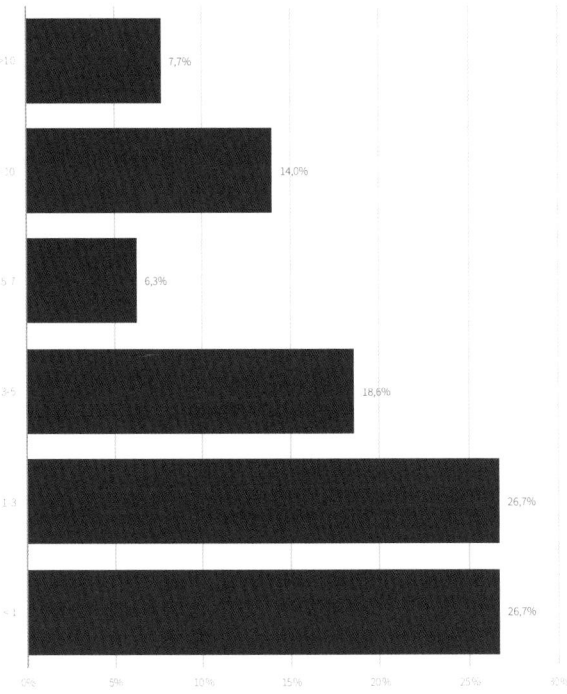

Figure 1.2: Personal Trainers in The Netherlands in terms of duration of being a Personal Trainer (in years).

In Figure 1.3, an overview is presented of the average monthly revenue per customer, for 2016, 2017 and 2018. Personal Trainers believe that the average revenue will increase. Overall the revenue is approximately 400 EUR per month per customer. Titze and Gronau (2015) reported that one full hour with a Personal Trainer in Germany is on average 89 EUR.

Figure 1.3: Monthly Personal Training revenue per customer, for 2016 - 2018 in The Netherlands.

Another outcome of the Dutch survey was the way Personal Trainers communicate with customers. See Table 1.2 for an overview.

Communication method	Never	Hardly	Average	Often	Always
WhatsApp	2.1%	4.3%	6.4%	46.8%	40.4%
Social Media	8.5%	4.3%	23.4%	34.0%	29.8%
Apps	26.7%	8.9%	6.7%	35.6%	22.2%
Phone	8.5%	6.4%	27.7%	38.3%	19.1%
Website	18.2%	20.5%	20.5%	22.7%	18.2%
SMS	44.4%	15.6%	13.3%	17.8%	8.9%
E-mails	10.9%	6.5%	37.0%	37.0%	8.7%
Newsletters	41.9%	11.6%	37.2%	2.3%	7.0%
Communication board	46.7%	15.6%	24.4%	11.1%	2.2%
Other	50.0%	0.0%	33.3%	16.7%	0.0%

Table 1.2: Methods of communication by Dutch Personal Trainers.

In another study, Middelkamp, Wolfhagen and Steenbergen (2015) conducted a European survey on fitness professionals and their focus on health behaviour change strategies. Of the participants, 11.7% were working for more than 15 years as a professional, 21.7% were categorised as fitness instructors, 45% as group fitness instructors, 93% as Personal Trainers and only 12% as exercise for health professionals (level 5). See Table 1.3.

Although most professionals scored only one option, multiple answers were possible, because professionals sometimes have multiple categories of registration. The largest group of fitness professionals (75%) charge money for one-to-one sessions of 60 minutes, followed by small group training (41.7%) and group fitness classes (38.3%).

Variable (* multiple answers possible)	Results
Age	38 (SD 10)
Females	56.7%
Professionals active in their first year	26.7%
Professionals active > 15 year	11.7%
Fitness instructor*	21.7%
Group fitness instructor*	45.0%
Personal Trainer*	93.0%

Table 1.3: Summary of data on participants in European survey.

About one third (38.5%) of the fitness professionals reported an average monthly revenue of less than 1,000 EUR. On the other side of the spectrum, 13.5% reported a turnover of over 5,000 EUR per month (excluding VAT), and 21% earned between 2,000 EUR and 3,000 EUR a month. Titze and Gronau (2015) found that the price of a trainer increases by experience. Personal Trainers that are less than 4 years in their profession charge 76 EUR per hour, Personal Trainers between five and nine years charge 87 and trainers that are over 10 years active invoice approx. 100 EUR per session.

These fees are substantially higher that US-based fees reported by IHRSA (2009). In their Guide to Personal Training, IHRSA communicates in-session hourly rates of fulltime Personal Trainers of USD 28. The fee of a specialty trainer is a bit higher, USD 33.

In 2010 and 2013, ACE conducted a survey of health and fitness professionals to better understand salary conditions in the sector. More than 3,000 ACE Personal Trainers, group fitness instructors, health coaches, and advanced health and fitness specialists responded.

In 2013, a Personal Trainer earned USD 52,000 per year (approx. 43,000 EUR), with an income per hour of approx. USD 26. From 2010 to 2013, the average income of parttime trainers increased by 12%. But, the income of fulltime Personal Trainers stayed the same. It is further notable that a fitness director in a club earns less income than a Personal Trainer (USD 48,000).

1.5 Activities of Personal Trainers

When Personal Trainer is considered as an umbrella term, the activities of Personal Trainer will automatically vary a lot. Many Personal Trainers execute physical training sessions with their customers. But what else do they do? What are their key activities?

Anderson et al. (2010) conducted the Canadian Personal Training survey. The study examined variability in service provision, knowledge and beliefs of Canadian Personal Trainers across levels of certification and education. All data were collected online over an eight-month period, and included demographical data, nutrition, weight management, physical activity, and general wellness knowledge, beliefs and common practice. Responses were scored based on their level of agreement with statements and their use of each item with their clients. The data were analysed according to the level of education of the participants.

Complete data were obtained for 268 fitness professionals: 9% secondary education, 19.2% one-year university, 18.0% college diploma and 53.9% university degree. Participants with more than a high-school diploma used the PAR-Q for pre-screening all the time. Those with a secondary school education usually promote high-fat diets and one-food-centred diets to lose body fat, while all education levels admitted to performing some type of nutritional counselling beyond the use of Canada's Food Guide.

The prescription of therapeutic exercise was common across all educational levels, with those with a diploma performing more of these activities than any other education level. The results suggested that many of the fitness professionals across all education levels work outside of their scope of practice, although this was more prevalent at lower educational levels.

The survey of Middelkamp et al. (2015), draws a picture on activities that fitness professionals (mainly Personal Trainers) charge money for. One-to-one sessions of 60 minutes are in the lead, followed by small group training (41.7%), and 38.3% charging for group fitness classes. See Figure 1.4.

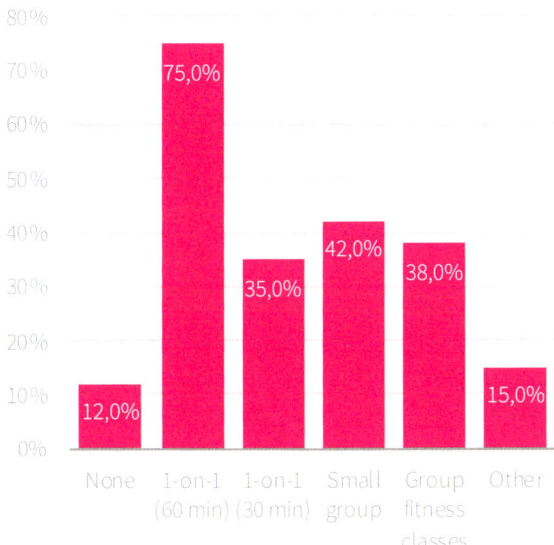

Figure 1.4: Overview of sessions for which fitness professionals do charge money.

The fitness professionals used a list of tools or activities to create interest (sell) with potential clients. The most used tool is a personal website, followed by business cards and referrals.

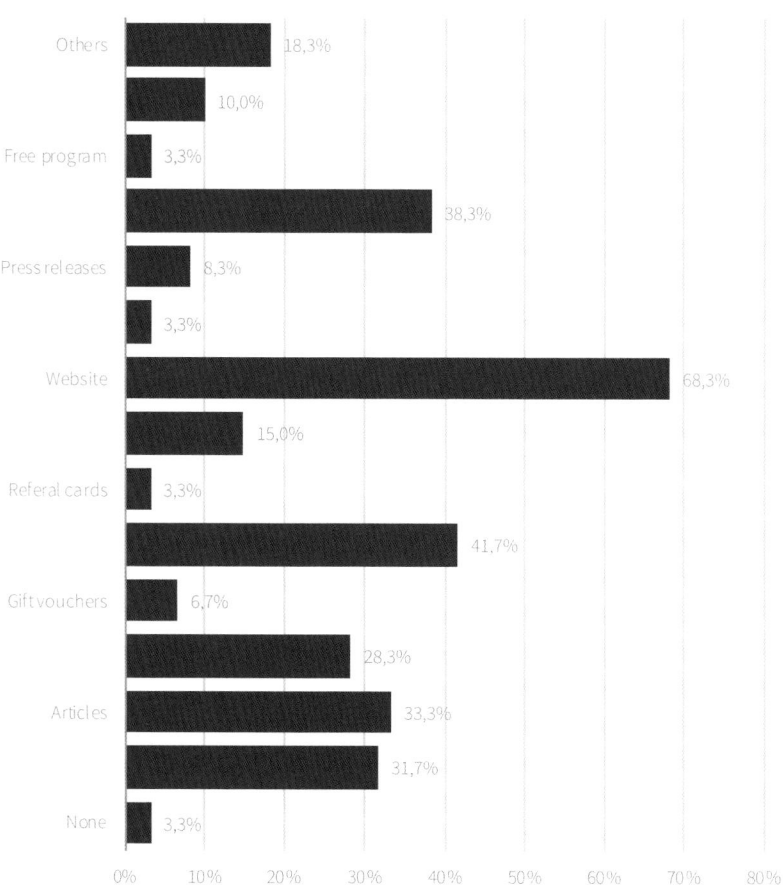

Figure 1.5: Tools used by Personal Trainers to create interest of clients.

With respect to health-behaviours (including physical activity, exercise, healthy eating, relaxation, limited sitting, non-smoking, sleeping) addressed by European fitness professionals (mainly Personal Trainers), Middelkamp et al. (2015) concluded that exercise was the most common form of health behaviour, with 86.7% of the participants in the survey offering this kind of service. Second, nutritional services are offered by 56.7%. The majority (91.7%) of the fitness professionals claimed that they addressed all-day physical activity in their programmes "often" or "all the time".

As far as relaxation and stress release are concerned, 36.7% of the fitness professionals registered that they included these health behaviours "all the time" in their programmes. Almost 12% of fitness professionals said that they "always" addressed all seven different health behaviours in their programmes. A total of 35.1% of these fitness professionals "always" took care of at least 4 different health behaviours in their programmes. And, 25.0% of the fitness professionals "often" or "always" addressed all seven different health behaviour determinants in their programmes. A large number (78.4%) of the fitness professionals "often" or "always" included at least four different health behaviours in their programmes. See Figure 1.6.

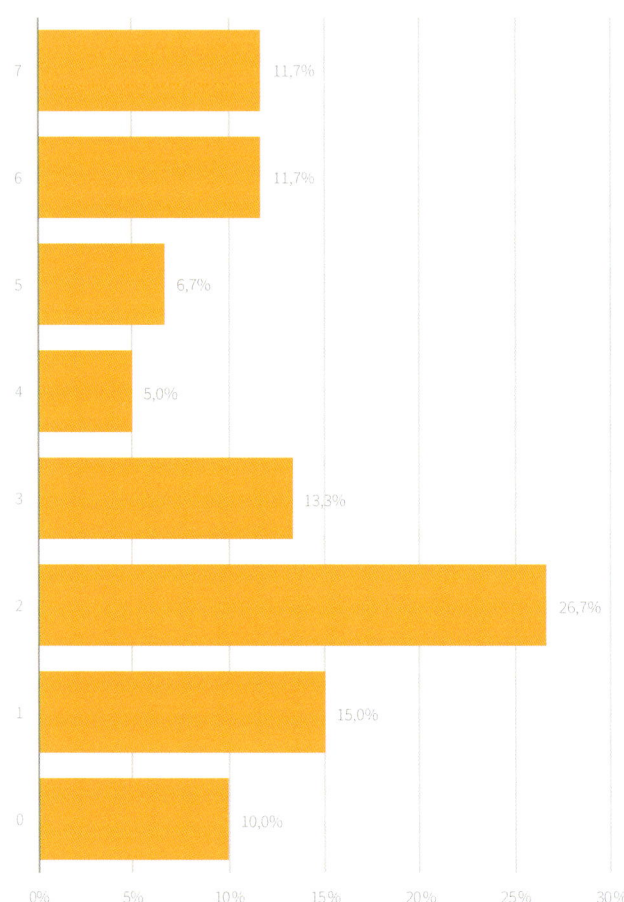

Figure 1.6: Number of health behaviours "always" addressed by Personal Trainers.

The survey was based on constructs of the transtheoretical model of behaviour change; including decisional balance, self-efficacy, processes of change, combined with the stage of change (pre-contemplation, contemplation, preparation, action, maintenance, relapse).

The most frequently used decisional balance strategy to increase behavioural change of potential clients (clients in the pre-contemplation, contemplation or preparation stage) focussed on the "useful benefits for the client", with 91.7% of the fitness professionals using this strategy. The only other strategy that was used by 50% of the fitness professionals was "useful losses for the client".

When confidence and beliefs of potential clients are concerned, "the client's belief regarding the perceived result of the outcomes of behaviour" is mostly used by the professionals. This strategy was used by 76.7% of the professionals, whereas 68.3% of the participants use "the confidence of the client to be engaged in positive behaviours". On the other hand, 28.3% of the participants use "the confidence of the client not to be engaged in negative behaviours".

Fitness professionals used strategies combined with practical tools, such as flyers or a personal website. The most frequently used tool to increase the interest of potential clients to participate was a website, focusing on the "useful benefits for the client". A total of 68.3% of the fitness professionals used this tool. Referral cards, press releases and seminars are less popular and only used by 10%.

1.6 Success factors of Personal Trainers

There are just a few studies available that investigate which skill-set fitness professionals require to support the needs of their customers and match certain industry quality criteria (Baart de la Faille, Middelkamp and Steenbergen, 2012). Overall, the standards focus mainly on topics like physiology, anatomy, injury prevention, energy systems, and different kinds of training. Less focus is placed on motivation and the promotion of behaviour change.

In a German study on Personal Trainers (Horn, 2011), a set of success factors for trainers was summarised by the trainers themselves. These are social competences, sympathetic look, capability, communicative skills, appearance and being a role model.

Two USA-based studies summarised similar success factors, including motivational skills, individuality (the ability of the trainer to give the customer a special feeling), emphatic ability and social skills (Melton, Katula and Mustian, 2008; Melton, Dail, Katula and Mustian, 2010). The focus on this kind of these so called "soft-skills" is becoming more apparent within fitness professionals and training providers.

For fitness professionals like Personal Trainers, skills to motivate and support clients on behaviour change have a double impact. First, it helps the clients to adapt and maintain health-related behaviours which results in higher levels of health and fitness. Second, in supporting clients on motivation and behaviour change, Personal Trainers can improve the levels of client (member) retention, which affects their business as a professional.

In the study of Melton et al. (2008; 2010), based on focus group discussion by Personal Trainers as well as Personal Training managers, the participants agreed that the appearance of one's physique was a critical consideration for clients hiring a Personal Trainer. The focus group members agreed by statements like "I think it's, unfortunately, it's huge. Other factors like gender or race and niche (being a specialist) are also mentioned as important. To achieve client loyalty, four factors are considered including motivational and social skills. See Figure 1.7.

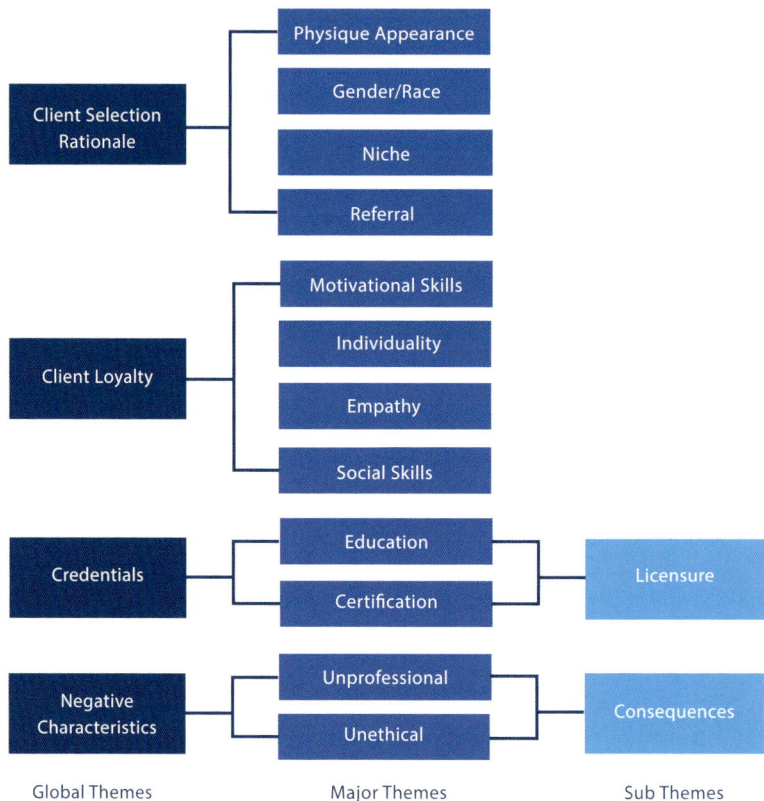

Figure 1.7: Hierarchy of themes for success in Personal Training (Melton et al., 2008; 2010).

According to a study performed in Austria, the average membership duration of members that train with a Personal Trainer is 3.77 years, compared to members that train without a Personal Trainer, at 2.96 years (Kronsteiner, 2010). However, it is unknown which factors deliver the positive correlation for Personal Training and retention.

1.7 Customers of Personal Trainers

Some data is available on customers or potential customers of Personal Trainers, based on published studies in Europe. Personal Trainers themselves know all details and profiles of their customers, of course, but a more general picture is scarce. A small study that provides information is a study by Kronsteiner (2010). The average age of the Personal Training customer is 43 years old. It is notable that members who train with a Personal Trainer are clearly older than members training without a Personal Trainer, 48 years old versus 37 years old.

In Horn's study (2011), 58% of the Personal Training customers belonged to the age group of 36-45 years. Merely 4% of customers were younger than 35 years old. In the Dutch survey (Middelkamp et al., 2017) 47% of the Personal Training customers were aged between 21 and 40, with a male-female ratio of 50-50.

Both in the study by Horn as in Kronsteiner's study, the largest group of customers of Personal Trainers consisted of entrepreneurs and self-employed earners. In Kronsteiner's study (2010), no less than 42% of the clientele was self-employed. This compared to 25% of the members that trained without a Personal Trainer.

Additionally, many customers are managers. A striking third group are the pensioners (11%). Among the Personal Training customers, 51% has a university education, compared to 43% of the non-

Personal Training customers in the same club. Unfortunately, little can be said about Personal Training in Europe in general on the basis of empirical research.

In the United States, IHRSA (2009) frequently reports on Personal Trainers and their customers. In the 2009 report, they provide a list of characteristics of clients: 68% appears to be a health club member; 57% female; 55% complete college or has an advanced degree; 53% has a household income higher than USD 100,000; 47% are veteran members; and 47% pays more to use a facility.

In the study of Middelkamp et al. (2015), the surveyed fitness professionals reported that the main goals clients mention at the start of a programme include: Losing weight (86.7%), getting fit (78.3%) and general improvement of health (75.0%). Titze and Gronau (2015) also state that weight loss is the number 1 motive of Personal Training clients (80% mentioned this motive), followed by body toning (muscles) (40%), rehabilitation (33%) and health (31%).

In Figure 1.8, an overview is presented of new Personal Training customers per year (Middelkamp et al., 2017). It is evident that Dutch Personal Trainers see a bright future ahead with a growing number of new clients.

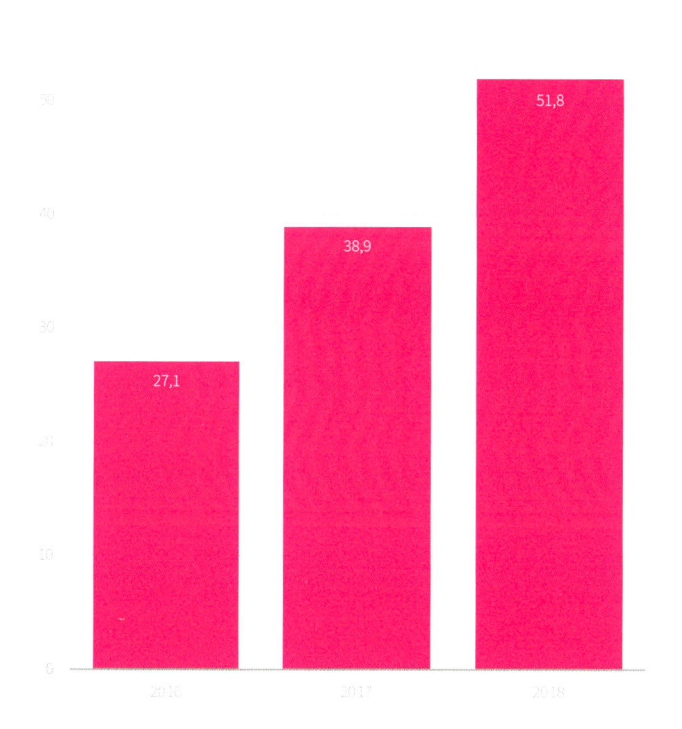

Bar chart showing values: 2016: 27,1; 2017: 38,9; 2018: 51,8.

Figure 1.8: Average number of new Personal Training customers per year.

In the same survey, it was reviewed how many customers per year quit with a Personal Trainer on average. Check out Figure 1.9.

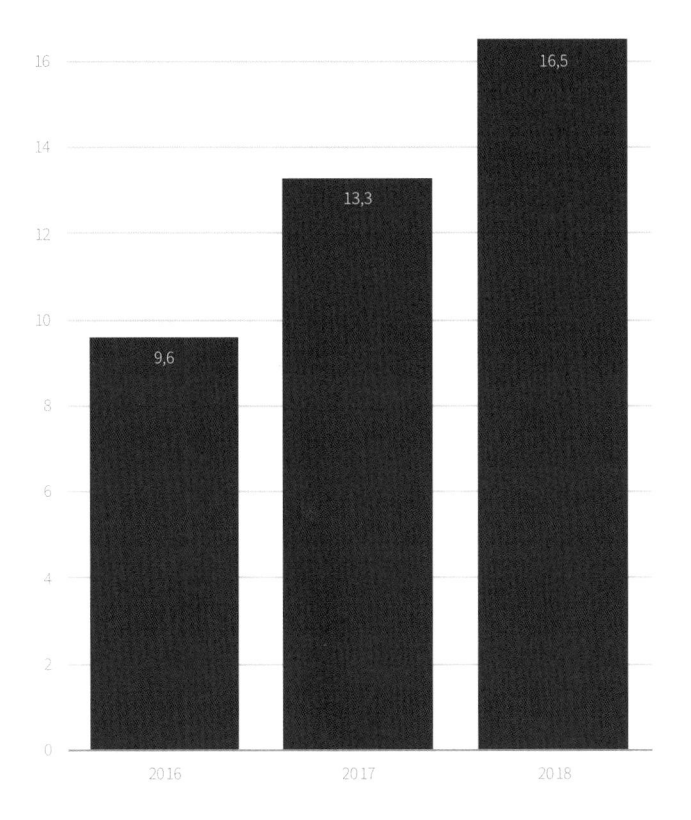

Figure 1.9: Average number of customers that stop with a Personal Trainer per year.

1.8 Personal Training studios

Another subject within Personal Training are Personal Training studios. Data on studios in Europe or globally is very limited. Below, a recent study on Personal Training studios in The Netherlands

(Middelkamp, Wolfhagen and Wouters, 2017) is summarised in Tables 1.4 and 1.5.

It is perhaps not that important to other countries how many studios there are in The Netherlands, but the growth ratio could be interesting. Of the studios counted in 2017, 66.6% has been open in the last 4.5 years. The capital city of Amsterdam counts 43 studios on a population of 853,000 inhabitants. In July 2017, the Netherlands has an estimated number of 623 Personal Training studios.

	PT studio's	Fit20	Curves	CrossFit	Total
10 biggest regions	125	22	7	50	204
Other parts	163	69	43	144	419
Total	288	91	50	194	623

Table 1.4: Overview of Personal Training studios in The Netherlands.

The Personal Training studios of the 10 biggest communities in The Netherlands were additionally interviewed on some Key Performance Indicators (KPIs), like customers per square meters or customers per trainer. See Table 1.5 for on overview of KPIs.

Items	Mean scores
Surface of studio	216m²
Number of active Personal Trainers	4.5
Number of active customers	99
Customers per square meter	0.42
Customers per Personal Trainer	22.4

Table 1.5: Overview KPIs of Personal Training studios in biggest regions of The Netherlands.

1.9 Conclusion

When reviewing this chapter, it can be concluded that a limited number of studies on Personal Training are published. The most consistent data available is on profiles of Personal Trainers, followed by profiles of customers. On other topics, many questions remain unanswered, for example on the effectiveness of Personal Training and client retention. When looking at data on profiles, activities, etcetera of Personal Trainers, many (European) countries are lacking with no studies yet found. Because studies demonstrated an irregular pattern it is difficult to discuss trends over time and long-term developments. For example, on the number of Personal Trainers per country or the growth of Personal Training studios. More studies are needed; the first will be published on the following pages.

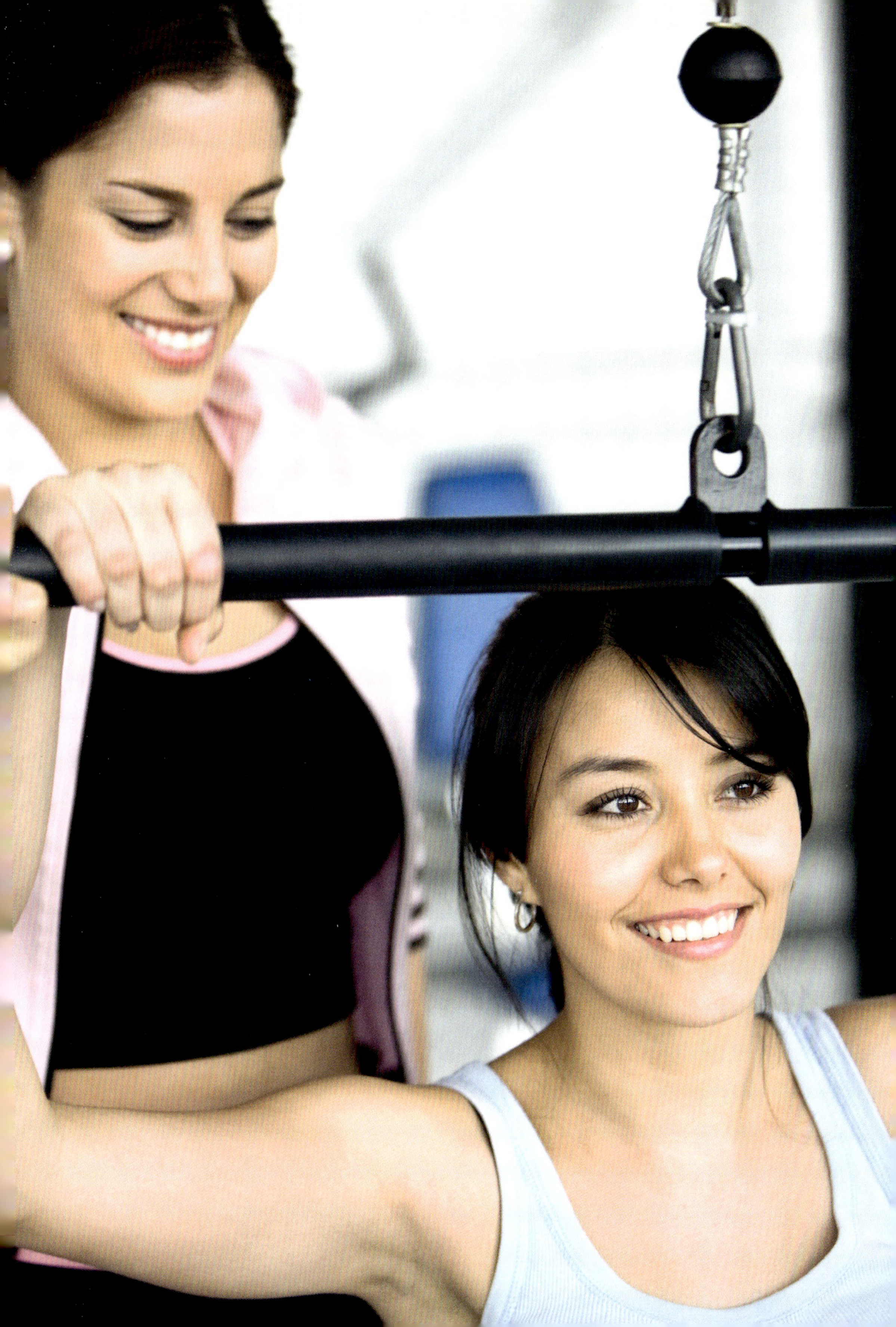

1.10 References

ACE (2010). Salary Survey Report 2010. American Councel on Exercise.

ACE (2013). Salary Survey Report 2013. American Councel on Exercise.

ACSM (2007). ACSM's Resources for the Personal Trainer, 2nd ed., Baltimore, ML: Lippincott Williams and Wilkins.

Anderson, G., Elliott, B., & Woods, N. (2010). The Canadian Personal Training survey. Journal of Exercise Physiology (Online), 13: 19-28.

EuropeActive (2011). EHFA Standards EQF Level 4 Personal Trainer. Brussels.

Horn, D. (2011). Personal Training in Deutschland; Daten, Fakten, Zahlen. Karlsruhe: Health and Beauty Business Media.

IBISWorld (2017). The Personal Trainers market research report. United Kingdom.

IHRSA (2009). IHRSA's Guide to Personal Training. International Health, Racquet and Sportsclub Association, Boston, USA.

Kronsteiner, M. (2010). Motivation für Personal Training im Fitnessstudio. Master's thesis, University of Vienna.

Melton, D.I., Dail, T.K., Katula, J.A., & Mustian, K.M. (2008). The current state of Personal Training: an industry perspective of Personal Trainers in a small Southeast community. Journal of Strength and Conditioning Research, 22 (3): 883-889.

Melton, D.I., Dail, T.K., Katula, J.A., & Mustian, K.M. (2010). The current state of Personal Training: managers' perspectives. Journal of Strength and Conditioning Research, 24 (11): 3173-3179.

Middelkamp J., & Willemsen, G. (Editors) (2010). Personal Training in Europa. Waalwijk.

Middelkamp, J., & Steenbergen, J. (2012). Personal training. In: Baart de la Faille, M., J. Middelkamp & J. Steenbergen (2012). The state of research in the global fitness industry. BlackBoxPublishers & EuropeActive, Brussels.

Middelkamp, J. (Editor) (2015). EuropeActive's Essentials of Motivation and Behaviour Change. EuropeActive, Brussels & BlackBoxPublishers, Nijmegen.

Middelkamp, J., Wolfhagen, P., & Steenbergen, B. (2015). The transtheoretical model and strategies of European fitness professionals to support clients in changing health-related behaviour: A survey study. Journal of Fitness Research, Volume 4, 3: 3-12.

Middelkamp, J. (2016). The role of the Personal Trainer; professionalism and presentation. Rieger, T., Jones, B., & Jimenez, A. (2016). Essentials for Personal Trainers. Human Kinetics.

Middelkamp, J, Wolfhagen, P., & Wouters, R. (2017). Personal Training in Nederland. BlackBoxPublishers, Den Bosch.

NSCA (2004). Uit: Baart de la Faille, M., Middelkamp, J., & Steenbergen, J. (2011; 2012). The state of research in the global fitness industry. BlackBoxPublishers, the Netherlands. Copied from NSCA website in 2011 (www.nsca.com).

Tharratt, S. & Rutgers, H. (2016). History of innovations in the fitness sector. In: Middelkamp, J. & Rutgers, H. (Editors). Growing the fitness sector through innovation. EuropeActive, Brussels, BlackBoxPublishers, Den Bosch.

Titze, G., & Gronau, N. (2015). Personal Training: Der Markt in Deutschland. Stand 2015. Edelhelfer, Mannheim.

US Bureau of Labor Statistics (2010). www.bls.gov.

MEET YOUR MOTIVATOR

WORKOUTS
FAT BURN
ENDURANCE
FITNESS →
SPEED
POWER

TomTom

Discover how fit you really are with Fitness Age

Get over 50 Personalised Workouts

Make every workout count with Multiple Sports Modes

SPARK 3

GPS FITNESS WATCHES

TOMTOM SPORTS

AVAILABLE ON TOMTOM SPARK AND TOMTOM SPARK 3 GPS FITNESS WATCHES WITH BUILT-IN HEART RATE MONITOR

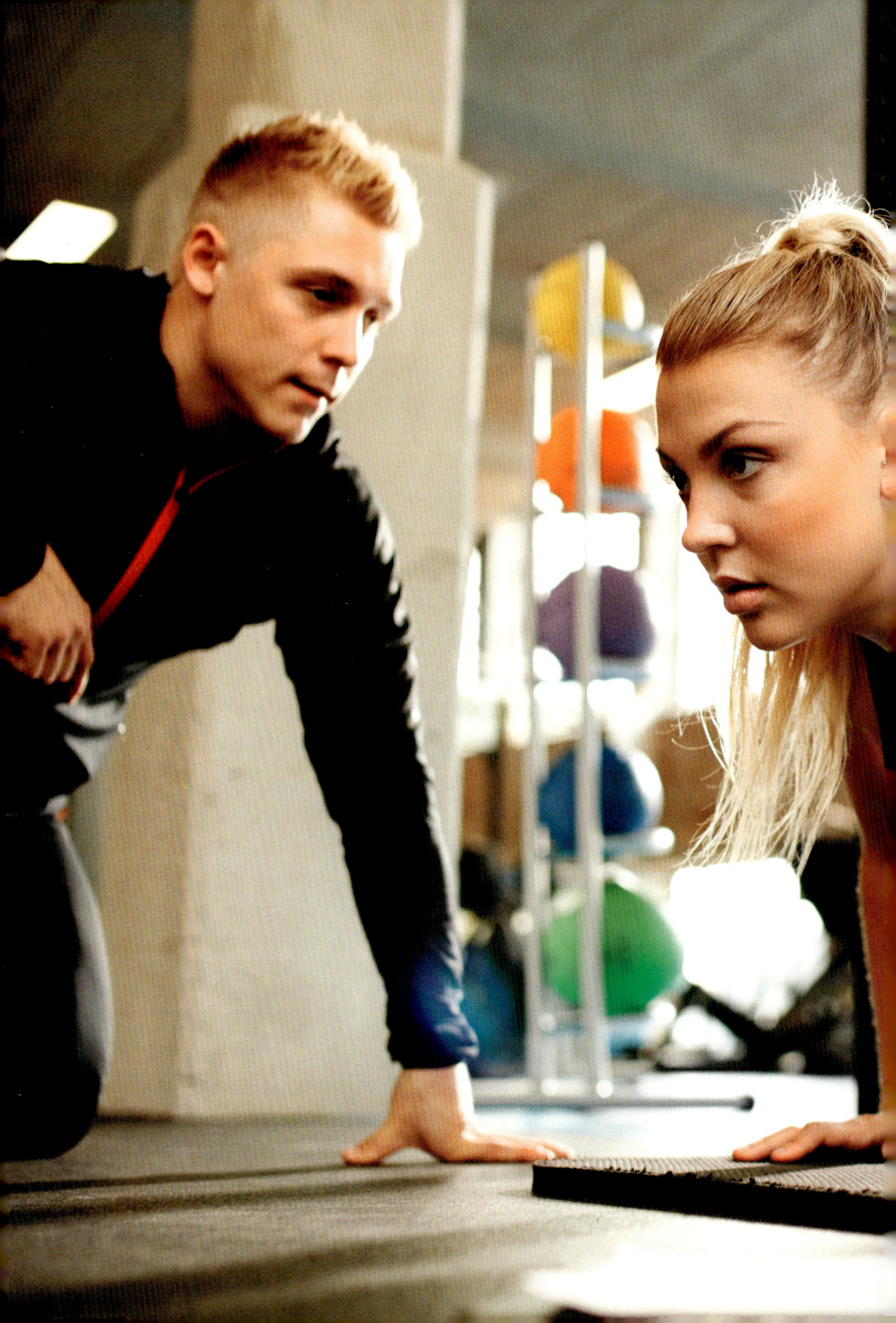

2

Personal Training Market Insights: An exploratory survey amongst European Personal Trainers

2. Personal Training Market Insights: An exploratory survey amongst European Personal Trainers

Niels Gronau
Niels Gronau is founder and managing director of the research and advisory boutique edelhelfer, which focuses its services solely on the sports and fitness industry.

Gregor Titze
Gregor Titze is the head of market research at edelhelfer and has been responsible for various reports especially on national as well as international fitness markets.

2.1 Introduction

When we started our initial research on Personal Training in Germany in 2015, we found little reliable information on this market segment of the health and fitness industry. While different publications already shed some light on the club operators' situation and development on a regular basis, only a limited number of publications dealt with the individual trainers working within a personal relationship with their clients. Amongst the few studies there are Freese (2006), Kieß (2007), and Horn (2009) analysed and commented on Personal Training in Germany in the last decade.

Nevertheless, not much data is available on the market size and structure of this segment.
Based on our previous national as well as international research in the general field of sports and fitness, we felt that Personal Training is an exciting and growing niche of the overall fitness market. More so, because in markets like the United States or the United Kingdom we see a high level of popularity and penetration of Personal Training offerings. Following a first glance into different Personal Training markets we found that the limited availability of information is similar across markets.

We therefore teamed up with EuropeActive, the European health and fitness association, to conduct an international research project on the state of Personal Training in 15 European countries. The countries in focus have been Austria, Belgium, Denmark, Finland, France, Germany, the United Kingdom, Ireland, Italy, Netherlands, Norway, Portugal, Spain, Sweden, and Switzerland. Those countries have been chosen as they represent the largest fitness markets in terms of membership numbers.

The core part of the research was an online questionnaire that was setup to cover a wide range of questions to be answered by fitness professionals and especially Personal Trainers, in their individual national languages. In addition, we targeted relevant major market players in the individual national markets such as associations, education providers or operators, to attempt to ascertain figures on the overall number of Personal Trainers and the operational structure of the segment in the respective markets.

Unfortunately, our first assessment has been confirmed: There is little knowledge in the individual markets with regard to the basic question of how many Personal Trainers there are currently offering their services. A major reason for this situation is that neither the term "Personal Training" is strictly defined nor "Personal Trainer" is a protected title. Hence, anyone offering for instance any kind of one-on-one training could call him- or herself a Personal Trainer in many countries. There is also a lack of clear organisation of Personal Training in some markets; some countries have a multitude of Personal Training associations, others have none.

2.2 Market size and Potential

To get at least an initial picture of the market size of Personal Training in different countries we have applied the numbers of the business- and employment-oriented social networking service LinkedIn. As of 31/12/2017 a total of 44,106 people stated that they are a Personal Trainer in their current job title. By far the largest market according to this approach is the United Kingdom with 22,678 Personal Trainers or 51.4% of the total amount of the 15 countries. Other countries with a comparably large number of Personal Trainers are Italy and the Netherlands. Denmark and Austria have the lowest number of Personal Trainers.

Country	No of Personal Trainers	LinkedIn penetration	Normalized No of Personal Trainers	Inhabitants per Personal Trainer
GB	22.678	34,4%	26.310	2.485
IT	6.048	17,0%	14.149	4.288
NL	4.076	39,9%	4.076	4.166
DE	1.885	8,5%	8.797	9.341
PT	1.876	19,8%	3.777	2.738
IE	1.557	28,4%	2.184	2.163
ES	1.372	20,7%	2.649	17.531
BE	793	23,8%	1.331	8.499
CH	693	23,8%	1.163	7.160
FR	685	21,7%	1.259	53.044
FI	679	15,7%	1.730	3.173
SE	641	25,7%	996	9.891
NO	492	26,0%	754	6.916
DK	319	32,6%	390	14.637
AT	312	10,9%	1.137	7.643
	44.106	23,3%	70.701	10.245

Table 2.1: Overview European Personal Training market.

Our attempt to approximate the respective market numbers obviously has its shortcomings. Not every Personal Trainer is present in this specific network and its penetration, i.e. the portion of LinkedIn members in the total population, differs between the individual countries. Moreover, the title "Personal Trainer" seems to have different levels of awareness and importance in the various relevant languages. For instance, in French the "coach sportif", in Spanish the "entrenador personal", or in Dutch the "persoonlijke trainer" are also used.

Another indication that the actual number of Personal Trainers might be even higher than the 44,106 in the 15 countries is the growth we have determined from 30/06/2017 until the end of the year. Coming from 42,000 LinkedIn members who stated to have the job title "Personal Trainer" as of the end of June, the growth rate until 31/12/2017 is almost 5%. As the social networking service has been able to enlarge its overall member base in Europe in the same time span, the increase of Personal Trainers seems to be predominately driven by the growing market penetration of LinkedIn in Europe.

Therefore, our approach should be recognised as exploratory. Nevertheless, we believe it is worthwhile as a starting point and call for additional research on this question. This should, then, be followed-up for each respective national situation.

To compare the individual national numbers and normalize the different penetration rates of LinkedIn, we have applied the highest national penetration seen in the Netherlands of 39.9% to all analysed countries. Taking this value as a basis, the total number of Personal Trainers in all countries would sum-up to 70,700. The biggest impact of this normalization procedure can be seen in Austria and Germany. The reason for the major differences between the collected number of Personal Trainers and the normalized values in these countries could be the strong presence of the German speaking professional network and LinkedIn competitor Xing.

Comparing the "normalized" numbers of Personal Trainers to the total population of the individual countries gives an indication of the number of inhabitants per Personal Trainer. This market indicator allows an assessment of the current national penetration of Personal Training as well as the free potential of each country. We find the lowest number of inhabitants per Personal Trainer in Ireland (2,163) and in the United Kingdom (2,485) which indicates a higher number of Personal Trainers and, thereby, a more developed market in these countries. In comparison, in France statistically more than 53,000 people share one Personal Trainer. Again, one reason for this exceptionally higher value might be that the title "Personal Trainer" is less common in France than in other countries.

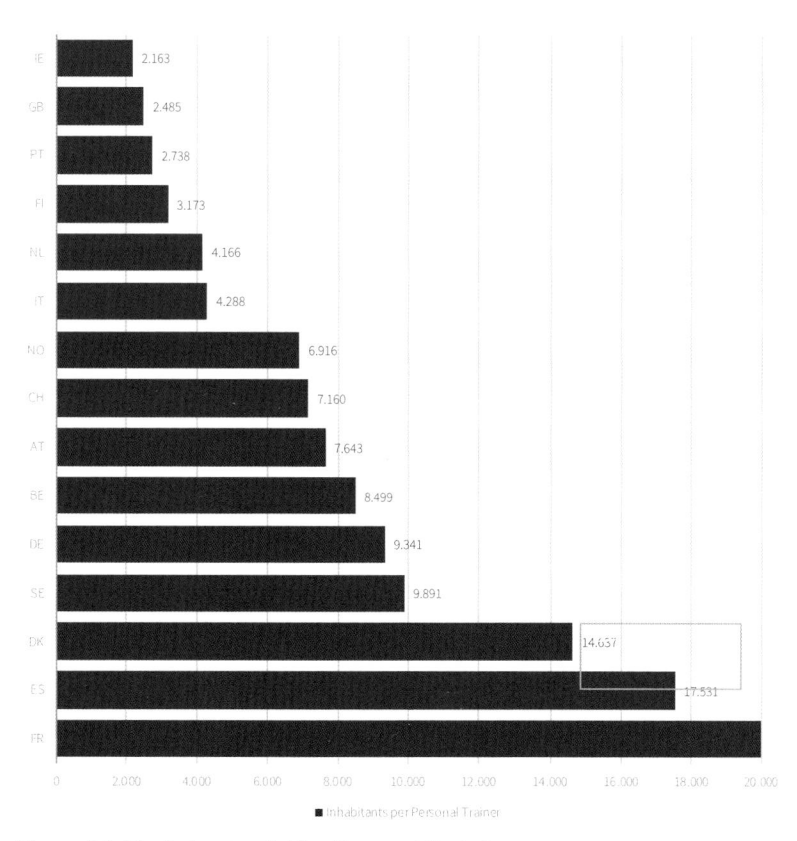

Figure 2.1: Market potential for Personal Training.

Even though the individual figures have to be interpreted carefully, they do allow a basic comparison between the different countries and an initial assessment of the European Personal Training market.

For our main analysis, a total of 4,370 fitness professionals participated in the online survey that has been online from June to September 2017. 3,944 of them are located in the focused 15 European markets, and 2,819 of these are Personal Trainers.

Country	All Participants	Personal Trainer	Share of Personal Trainers
IT	646	500	77,4%
GB	466	352	75,5%
DE	381	302	79,3%
FI	321	226	70,4%
NL	233	184	79,0%
ES	420	175	41,7%
DK	219	161	73,5%
AT	219	147	67,1%
BE	164	137	83,5%
PT	148	118	79,7%
IE	150	109	72,7%
NO	123	105	85,4%
FR	159	104	65,4%
SE	138	101	73,2%
CH	157	98	62,4%
Total	3.944	2.819	71,5%

Table 2.2: Survey participation.

By far the strongest participation in total numbers was achieved in Italy where 500 Personal Trainers took part in our survey. Second-ranked is the United Kingdom with 352 participating Personal Trainers. However, considering the total number of more than 26,000 Personal Trainers in the United Kingdom, the participation rate is only 1.3%; by far the lowest of all 15 countries.

The highest rate has been achieved in Denmark where based on the LinkedIn numbers, 41.3% of all Personal Trainers took part. The average participation rate across countries is 9.7%. Even in Switzerland, the country with the lowest absolute number of participating Personal Trainers, it is still as high as 98.

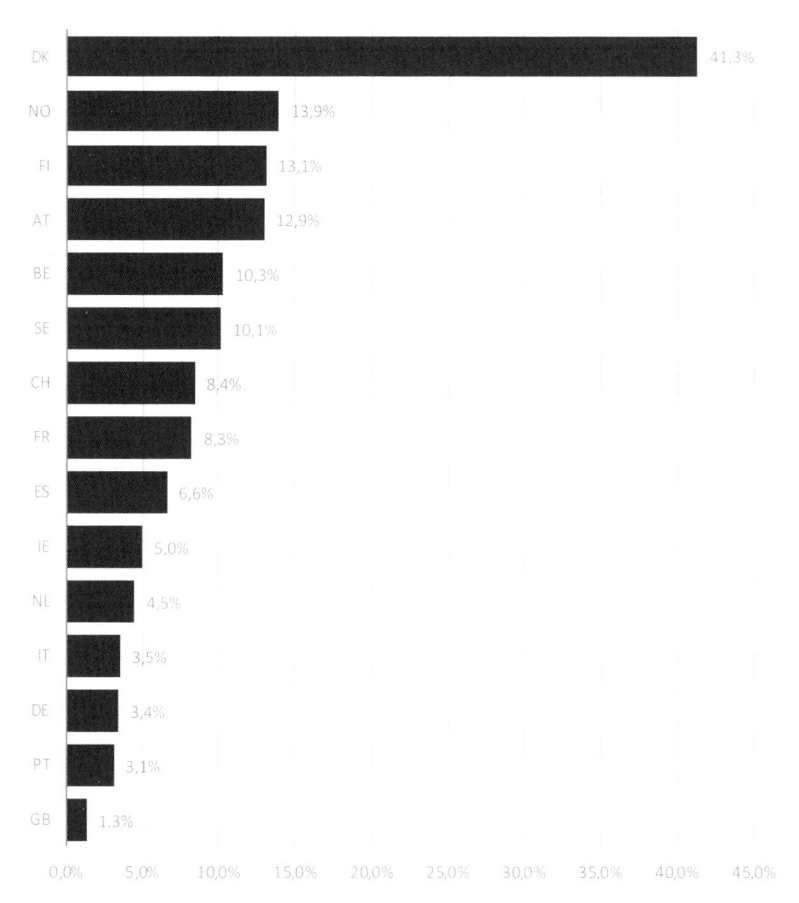

Country	Rate
DK	41,3%
NO	13,9%
FI	13,1%
AT	12,9%
BE	10,3%
SE	10,1%
CH	8,4%
FR	8,3%
ES	6,6%
IE	5,0%
NL	4,5%
IT	3,5%
DE	3,4%
PT	3,1%
GB	1,3%

Figure 2.2: Participation rates per country.

Our survey contained a wide range of questions providing a detailed picture of the situation of Personal Trainers in the analysed countries. The survey covered topics from Personal Trainers' characteristics to details of their operations or issues related to their clients to aspects concerning the overall market.

2.3 Personal Trainer characteristics

The most basic characteristic of a Personal Trainer is the gender. In our survey, 2,817 trainers answered this initial question. On average, 63.8% of these participants are male and 36.1% female. We also allowed the classification "others", which was chosen, however, by only 4 participants or 0.1%. The higher portion of male Personal Trainers was especially impacted by the situation in Italy, where more than 80% of the Personal Trainers are men.

Comparable but less significant is the distribution in the other two southern European countries Spain (74.3%) and Portugal (69.5%). All three Southern European countries are historically known to be more masculine societies. A little bit more surprising is the situation in Belgium where three-quarters of the participating Personal Trainers are male.

Country	Female	Male
FI	59,7%	40,3%
NO	51,4%	48,6%
AT	47,6%	52,4%
FR	46,2%	53,8%
DK	45,3%	54,7%
SE	44,6%	55,4%
CH	41,8%	58,2%
IE	38,5%	60,6%
NL	37,0%	63,0%
DE	36,4%	63,6%
GB	36,4%	63,6%
PT	30,5%	69,5%
ES	25,1%	74,3%
BE	24,1%	75,9%
IT	18,5%	81,1%

■ female ■ male ■ other

Figure 2.3: Distribution of gender.

The highest portion of female Personal Trainers is achieved in Finland with 59.7%, followed by another Scandinavian country, namely Norway. However, these two are the only markets with a majority of female Personal Trainers.

In the thirteen other countries the portion of male trainers is higher and in some even significantly higher as shown before. It will be interesting to see whether the share of female Personal Trainers in the individual fitness markets will increase in the future.

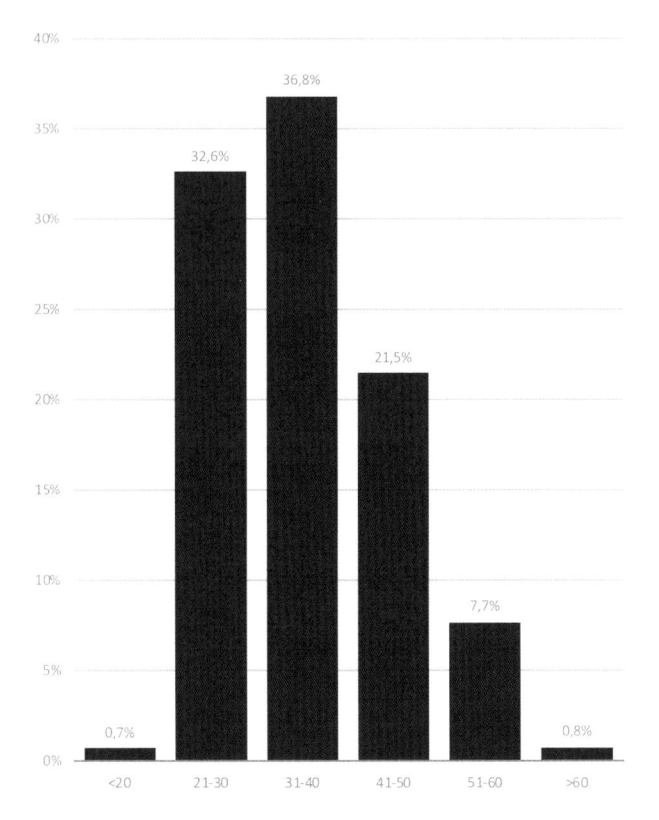

Figure 2.4: Distribution of age (in years).

A second initial parameter is the Personal Trainers' age. When looking at the distribution of age groups amongst Personal Trainers, it becomes obvious that trainers are a rather young group of professionals. A total of 70.1% are 40 years old or younger and one third is a maximum of 30 years old. The number of trainers drops considerably beyond 40 years. Only 21.5% of the trainers are in the range between 41 to 50 years and only 7.7% in the 51 to 50 cluster.

Two major factors might influence this distribution. On the one hand, Personal Training itself is a rather "young" offering that is still developing and, therefore, not so many "older" people are engaged in the profession. On the other hand, Personal Training is mostly related to doing sports and being active within the role of a trainer. Therefore, it tends to be practiced rather by younger professionals and for a shorter time period than other jobs.

However, when considering older client groups and understanding the Personal Trainer role more as a life coach than a fitness instructor, Personal Training could develop more into a profession that is also attractive for older age groups in future years.

Today though, the average age of 34 for Personal Trainers in the analysed 15 countries is rather low. This average age ranges from 31 years in Norway to 37 in Finland and Switzerland.

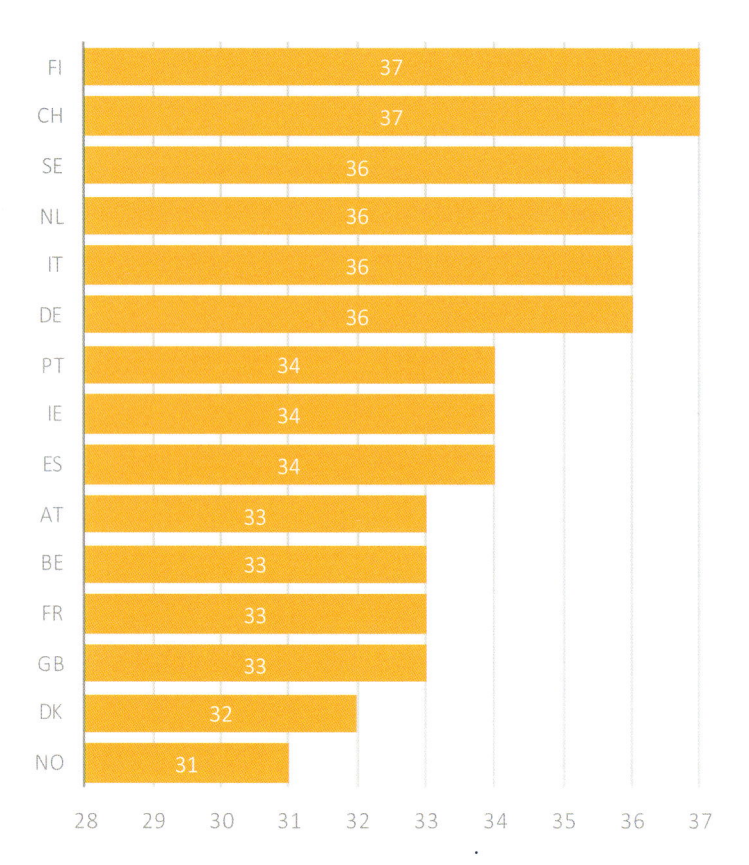

Country	Age
FI	37
CH	37
SE	36
NL	36
IT	36
DE	36
PT	34
IE	34
ES	34
AT	33
BE	33
FR	33
GB	33
DK	32
NO	31

Figure 2.5: Average age per country (in years).

Another interesting aspect of our survey is the question of where Personal Trainers work in terms of the size of their place of work. Based on the data received, major cities seem to record a strong share of the overall number of Personal Trainers.

As an international average almost one third of the participating trainers work in cities with more than 500,000 inhabitants. Metropoles with a population larger than 1,000,000 alone are home to 20.1% of all Personal Trainers. The largest portion of Personal Trainers in cities with more than 500,000 inhabitants is seen in Austria, Spain, and Germany.

Given the fact that Austria has only one city with more than 1,000,000 inhabitants, 51% of the participating Austrian Personal Trainers work in Vienna. A similar situation of a low concentration on larger cities is also seen in Belgium, the Netherlands, and Switzerland, where 30% of the Personal Trainers work in cities with less than 25,000 inhabitants; by far the highest figure of all countries.

Figure 2.6: Location of work per city size.

These findings call for a more detailed investigation. The analysis becomes more meaningful when the distribution of Personal Trainers is compared to the general population in the individual categories of the city sizes. For Germany, for instance, it becomes evident that Personal Trainers seem to be concentrated in the larger cities. While only 20.1% of the total German population live in cities with more than 250,000 inhabitants, more than 50% of the Personal Trainers work in these communities. On the other side, 46.8% of the population live in cities smaller than 25,000 inhabitants, where only 15% of the Personal Trainers work.

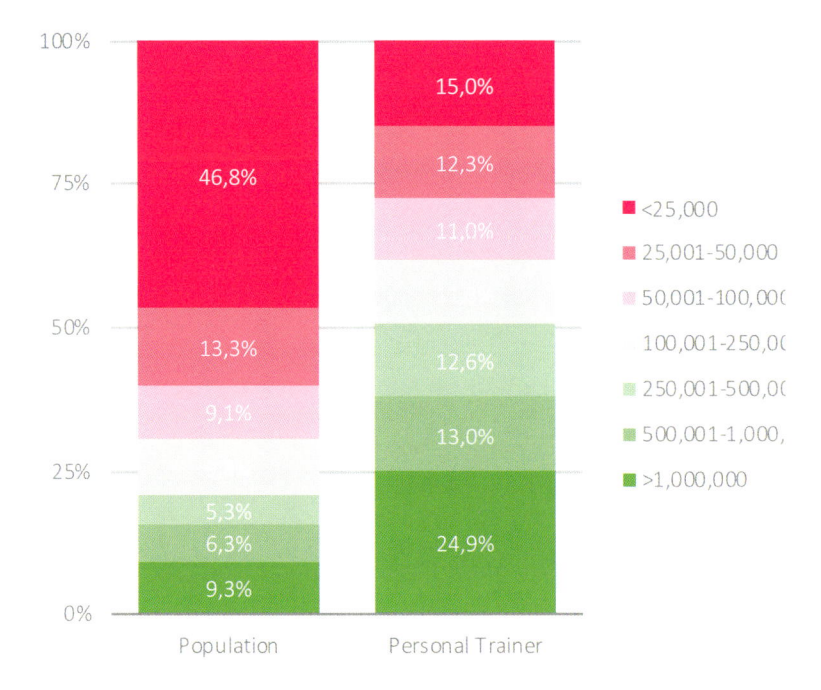

Figure 2.7: Comparison Personal Trainer to total population (in Germany).

The essential reason for this concentration of Personal Trainers is surely the higher absolute presence of the relevant target group in the larger cities. Therefore, it seems unlikely that this relationship will differ significantly between the individual markets or that it will change significantly as the Personal Training market develops.

An important aspect of the survey was to ascertain why someone has chosen to work as a Personal Trainer. A wide range of motivations from extrinsic factors like earning money to intrinsic parameters such as helping people or turn hobby into a career are potential reasons to start this specific profession.

Our results show that the most important motivation for 76.3% of the participants is the general interest in sports and fitness, followed by helping people (61.9%), and turning hobby into a career (61.1%). Only one quarter of the participants named making money as their key motivation to begin working as a Personal Trainer.

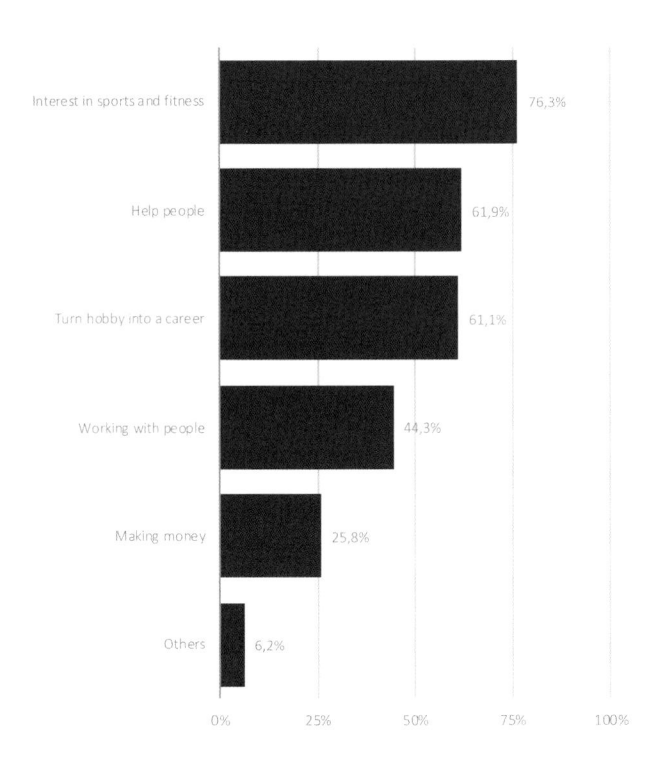

Figure 2.8: Motivation to start working as a Personal Trainer.

Knowing why someone has started to work in this field, it might also be interesting to know how satisfied they are with their decision and their work as a Personal Trainer. The "happiest" trainers are based in the Netherlands, Germany, and Austria indicating the two best scores in the six-points satisfaction scale. 85% of the Dutch Personal Trainers seem to be happy with their job. The highest portion of the very satisfied trainers work in Switzerland, where 55.6% rated their level of satisfaction in this way, followed by Austria and Germany.

In contrast, only 22.2% of the Personal Trainers in Portugal rate their job satisfaction with the most positive category. However, the overall level of "happiness" seems to be high amongst Personal Trainers. Only a very limited portion state they are not satisfied or even not at all satisfied. The highest share of Personal Trainers with the lowest level of satisfaction is again seen in Portugal with 2.8%, the United Kingdom with 2.6%, and Italy with 1.6%.

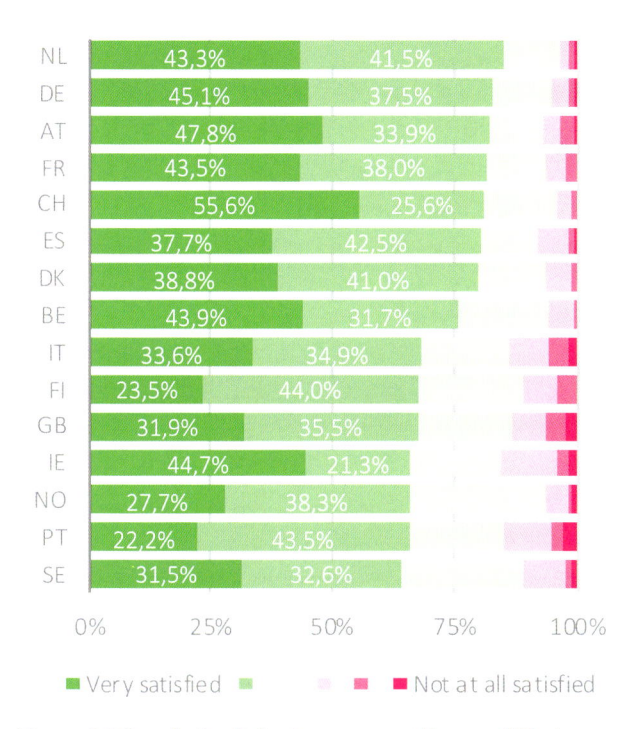

Country	Very satisfied				Not at all satisfied
NL	43,3%	41,5%			
DE	45,1%	37,5%			
AT	47,8%	33,9%			
FR	43,5%	38,0%			
CH	55,6%	25,6%			
ES	37,7%	42,5%			
DK	38,8%	41,0%			
BE	43,9%	31,7%			
IT	33,6%	34,9%			
FI	23,5%	44,0%			
GB	31,9%	35,5%			
IE	44,7%	21,3%			
NO	27,7%	38,3%			
PT	22,2%	43,5%			
SE	31,5%	32,6%			

Figure 2.9: Level of satisfaction amongst Personal Trainers.

The most important reason for this generally high satisfaction level is seen in the possibility to help people. 61.9% of all participants stated that this has a very positive impact on their happiness in their job, followed by fun of working in the field of sports, and the potential for development. Again only 20.7% state that making money is a source of satisfaction in what they are doing.

The strongest negative impact amongst trainer activities is the related administrative work for Personal Trainers together with selling to potential clients.

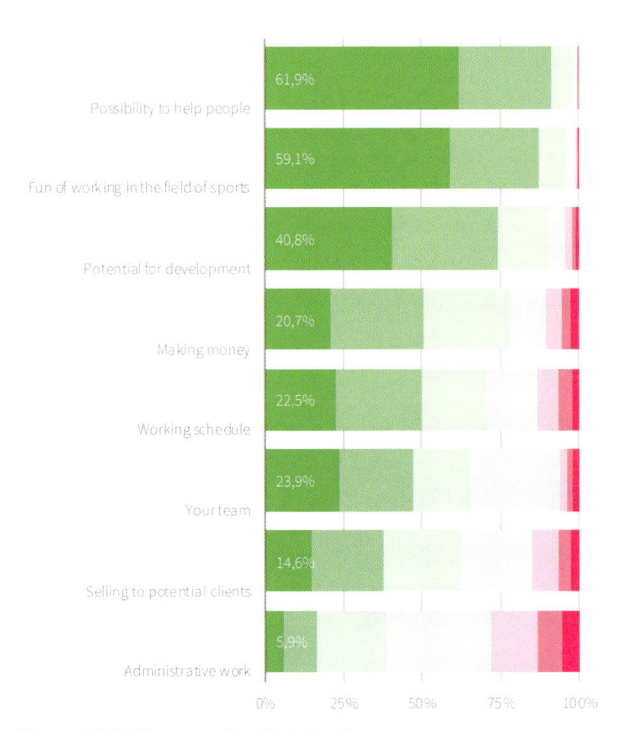

Figure 2.10: Reasons for Satisfaction.

Looking at the time participants have spent in their role as Personal Trainers as well as generally in the health and fitness industry, it becomes evident that the timeframes are rather small.

Almost two thirds (65.0%) of the participating trainers have worked for a maximum of five years as Personal Trainers; another 19.2% for six to ten years. Together, 84.2% have a maximum of ten years of experience in their job, which means that only 15.8% have more than these ten years. Only 6.9% of all participating Personal Trainers have more than 15 years of job experience.

The numbers change slightly if the time spent in the industry so far is queried. In this case, 64.1% of the participants state that they have been in the industry for a maximum of ten years. This longer industry experience could be explained by other industry jobs that have been pursued before working as a Personal Trainer. Still, the portion of Personal Trainers with experience of not more than five years is, at almost half (47.7%) of the Personal Trainers, comparably high.

Personal Training Market Insights: An exploratory survey

```
                 In the fitness undustry    As a Personal Trainer
    0-5              47,7%                      65,0%
    6-10             16,4%                      19,2%
    11-15            15,5%                       8,9%
    16-20            10,6%
```

■ 0-5   ■ 6-10   ■ 11-15   ■ 16-20   ■ 21-25   ■ >25

Figure 2.11: Time spent in the industry and as a Personal Trainer (in years).

After answering the question of how many years someone has spent in their profession, it is also useful to know their current working hours. In this respect, a differentiation between fulltime and parttime Personal Trainers could be very helpful.

Based on our survey, these two types of employment seem to be relatively evenly distributed in the industry. Over all 15 countries, 46.3% of the Personal Trainers work fulltime, while 53.7% of them are engaged on a parttime basis.

An even more balanced picture is shown when looking at male Personal Trainers only. While 50.9% of men work fulltime 49.1% are active parttime. For female Personal Trainers the situation differs significantly. Only 38.1% of them work fulltime while 61.9% work parttime.

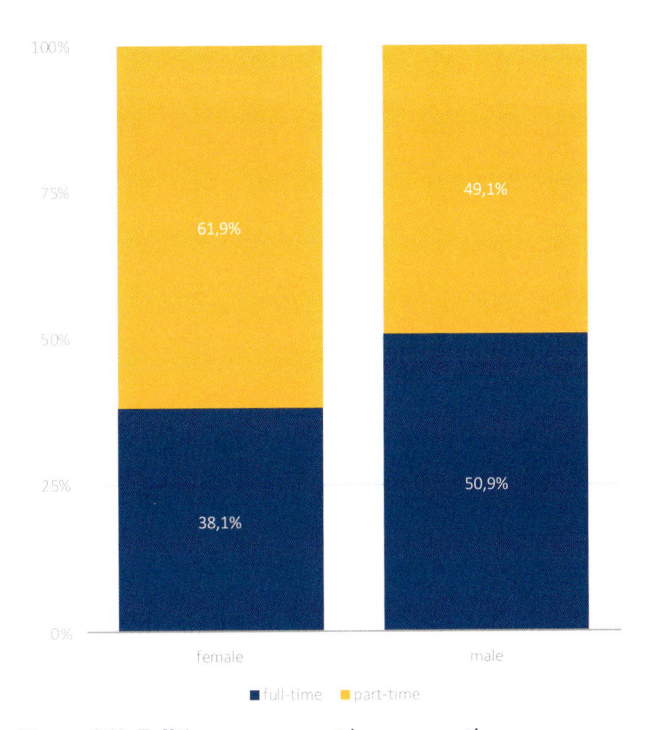

Figure 2.12: Fulltime versus parttime occupation.

As already seen in the total numbers of Personal Trainers, of which almost two-thirds actually are men, those women working as a Personal Trainer do so rather on a parttime basis.

Even though the international average is equally distributed between full- and parttime engagement, it differs significantly on a national level. While in the United Kingdom almost 60% of the Personal Trainers work fulltime, the portion is only 27.6% in Sweden.

It is interesting that also in the other two Scandinavian countries Denmark and Finland the share of fulltime trainers is with 32.1% below and with 33.9% at one third of all Personal Trainers. However, the portion of fulltime Personal Trainers in Norway, the fourth country in Scandinavia, with 57.1% is the second largest after the United Kingdom.

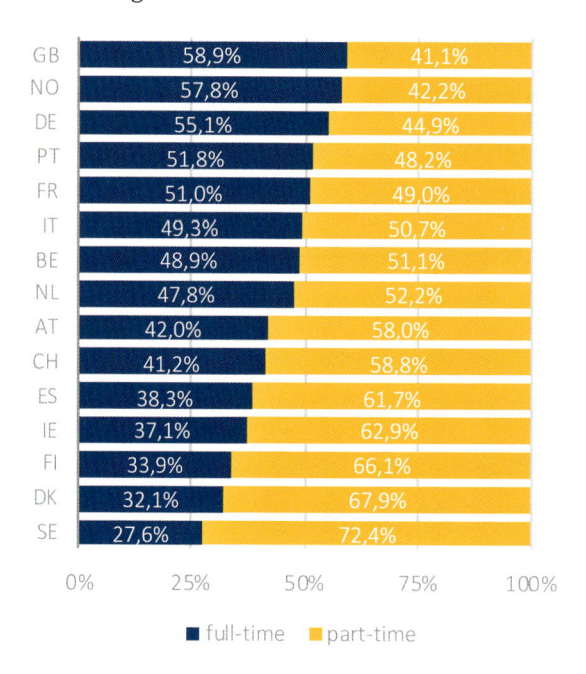

Country	full-time	part-time
GB	58,9%	41,1%
NO	57,8%	42,2%
DE	55,1%	44,9%
PT	51,8%	48,2%
FR	51,0%	49,0%
IT	49,3%	50,7%
BE	48,9%	51,1%
NL	47,8%	52,2%
AT	42,0%	58,0%
CH	41,2%	58,8%
ES	38,3%	61,7%
IE	37,1%	62,9%
FI	33,9%	66,1%
DK	32,1%	67,9%
SE	27,6%	72,4%

Figure 2.13: Fulltime versus parttime occupation by country.

Beyond the general classification in full- and parttime occupation, we have also requested the actual maximum number of hours per week they are available for Personal Training from the participants in our survey. Thereby, almost three-quarters of the Personal Trainers state to be available between five to 30 hours per week. Only 17.4% are available more than 30 hours and an availability of less than five hours is offered only by 9.2% of the participants.

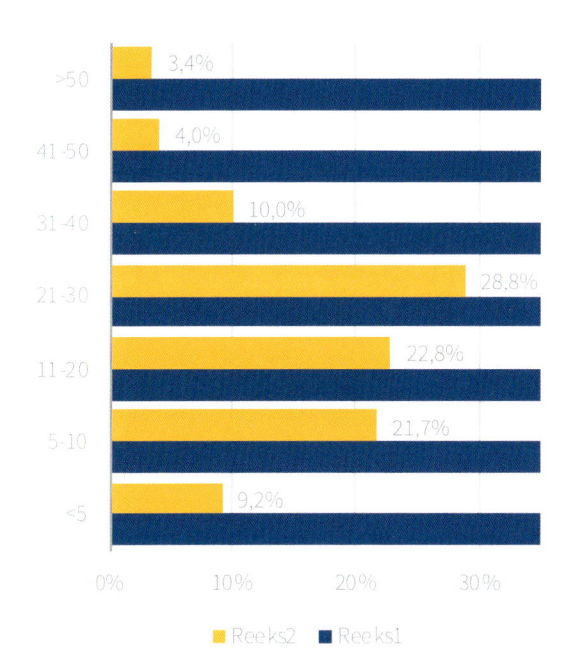

Hours	%
>50	3,4%
41-50	4,0%
31-40	10,0%
21-30	28,8%
11-20	22,8%
5-10	21,7%
<5	9,2%

Figure 2.14: Availability for Personal Training (hours per week).

On average, the participating Personal Trainers have a maximum availability of 21.4 hours per week. As it is to be expected, these numbers differ when splitting into fulltime and parttime. Fulltime

Personal Trainers state to have a total weekly availability of 26.2 hours on average. In contrast, parttime trainers state to have 15.6 hours per week. These number vary significantly also between the individual countries.

The participating fulltime Personal Trainers in Portugal answer to have a maximum time of 36 hours in which they are available for Personal Training sessions, followed by Norway (35 hours) and Sweden (34 hours). The lowest availability of fulltime Personal Trainers is seen in Finland (24 hours), Ireland (26 hours) or Austria (26 hours).

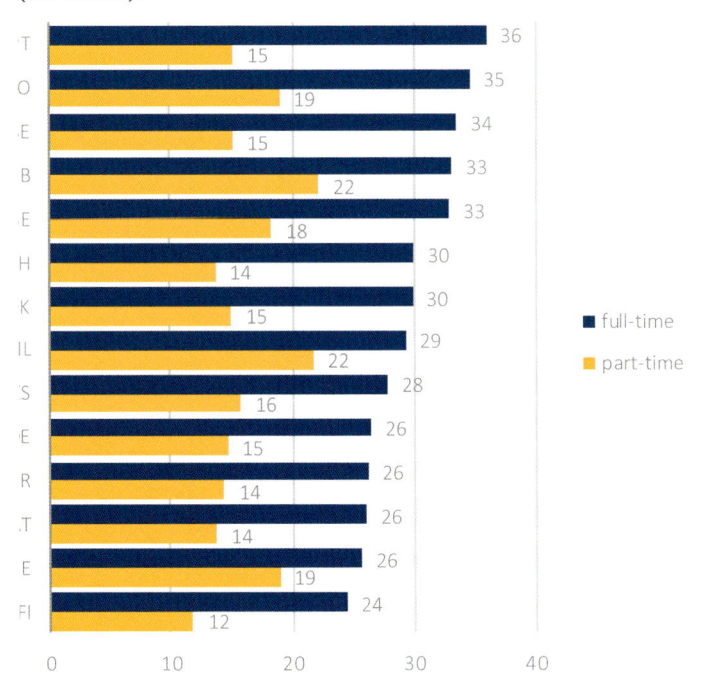

Figure 2.15: Availability for Personal Training by country (hours per week).

With respect to parttime Personal Trainer, the availability for a Personal Training session range from 12 hours on average in Finland to 22 hours in the Netherlands as well as in the United Kingdom. Based on the respective "capacity" for Personal Trainer sessions, it is also interesting to see how they actually spend and distribute their working time.

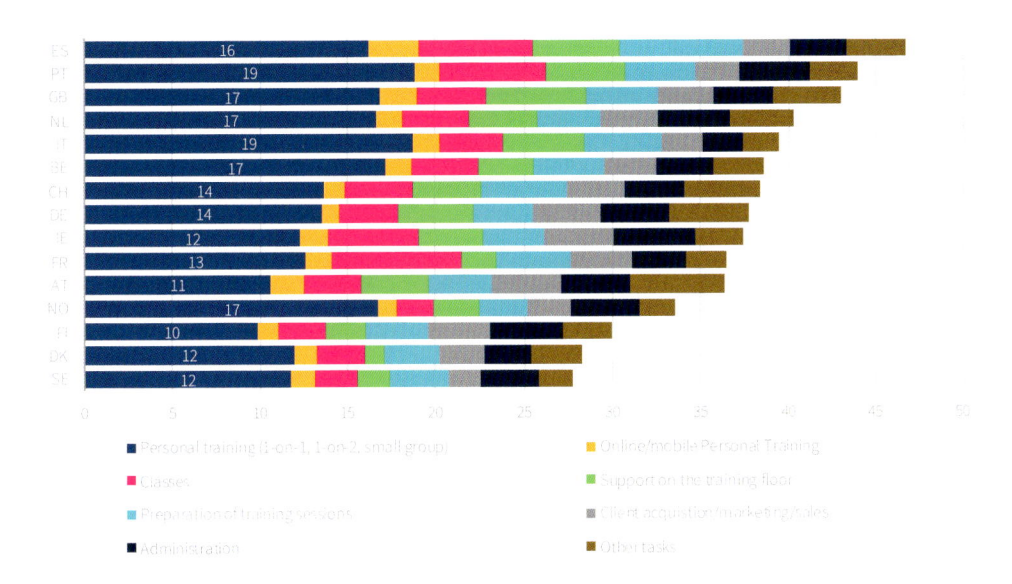

Figure 2.16: Distribution of working hours per week.

The two countries with the highest workload based on our survey are Spain and Portugal with a total number of 47 and 44 hours respectively. Thereof, the trainers give on average 16 Personal Training sessions in Spain and 19 in Portugal.

The portion of the effective Personal Training session at the total work to be done varies between the individual countries from almost 30% to more than 50%. Most efficient are thereby obviously the trainers in Norway, who manage to have Personal Training sessions in more than half of their working time. In contrast, Personal Trainers in Austria only have respective sessions in 29% of their time.

Other services offered by Personal Trainers are online or mobile Personal Training, giving classes, support on the training floor. In addition, Personal Trainers have to complete tasks like preparation of training sessions, acquisition of clients or administrative work. So far, online or mobile Personal Training only plays a role for a minority of 3 to 6 % of the Personal Trainers.

With respect to our survey, Personal Trainers in the three Scandinavian countries Finland, Denmark, and Sweden work the least with average working hours of 28 to 33. One reason for this situation should be the comparable high portion of parttime Personal Trainers in these three countries.

Another key segmentation parameter for the Personal Training market besides individual working time is the differentiation into employed and self-employed trainers. Almost three-quarters of the nearly 3,000 Personal Trainers who answered the relevant question work self-employed; more precisely, 73.1% of them are self-employed.

Thereby, the difference between women and men is not as significant as in their employment status. While the gap was 12 percentage points in the fulltime status, it is only 5 percentage points with regard to self-employment, which means that 74.6% of male and 69.9% of female Personal Trainers are self-employed. Approximately 7% indicate working in both categories.

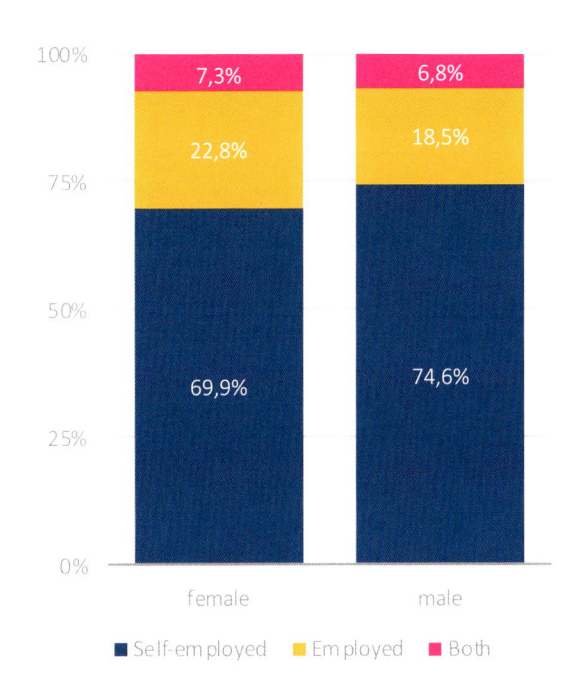

Figure 2.17: Employed versus self-employed occupations.

Comparable to the differentiation in full- and parttime working, also the employment status differs strongly between the individual countries. More than 90% of the participants in Belgium stated that they are working self-employed as a Personal Trainer. The second and third highest share is seen in the United Kingdom and Austria, each with more than 80% self-employed trainers.

In the three Scandinavian countries Norway, Sweden, and Denmark the portion of self-employed Personal Trainers ranges between only 36.9% and 55.8%.

Country	Self-employed	Employed	Both
BE	92,5%		5,2%
GB	82,2%	13,7%	
AT	80,2%	13,7%	
DE	79,9%	12,6%	
NL	78,3%	15,6%	
OT	76,7%	16,7%	
PT	75,4%	18,4%	
FR	75,0%	7,0%	18,0%
FI	74,9%	19,6%	
CH	74,2%	18,6%	
IE	67,0%	26,4%	
ES	62,7%	30,8%	
DK	55,8%	34,6%	
SE	50,0%	39,8%	
No	36,9%	57,3%	

Figure 2.18: Employed versus self-employed occupations by country.

It is noteworthy that the portion of those Personal Trainers working in both employment categories in France is significantly the highest with 18%.

This report only gives an initial understanding of the market conditions in the individual countries. It will need further, consecutive research with a detailed focus on the respective countries to elaborate the specific conditions for Personal Trainers that lead to the different offering structures.

A highly relevant information is usually the potential and actual level of income that could be realized within an industry. Therefore, we have questioned this field of information also in our survey amongst Personal Trainers. Unfortunately, the number of employed Personal Trainers who shared their information concerning their personal salary situation has been too low to achieve reliable results for every country. This is especially the case due to the majority of Personal Trainers working self-employed.

For this group of self-employed Personal Trainers, we have reliable and comparable data of their income or revenue situation.

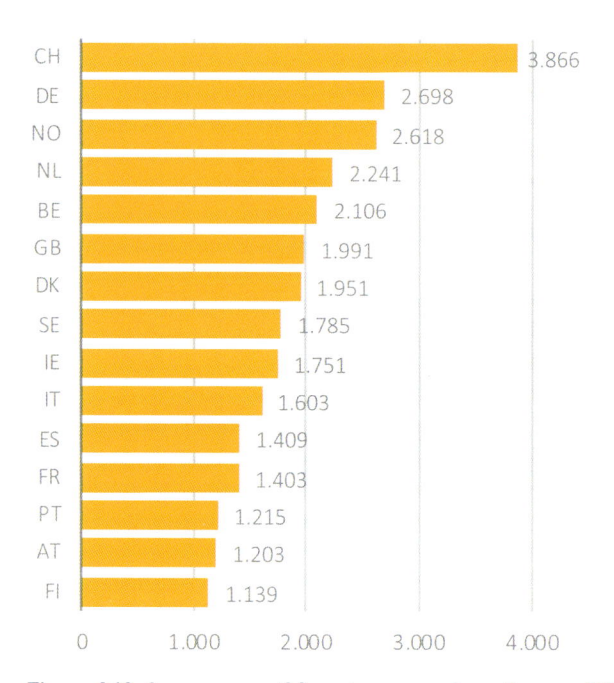

Country	Avg. monthly net revenue (EUR)
CH	3.866
DE	2.698
NO	2.618
NL	2.241
BE	2.106
GB	1.991
DK	1.951
SE	1.785
IE	1.751
IT	1.603
ES	1.409
FR	1.403
PT	1.215
AT	1.203
FI	1.139

Figure 2.19: Average monthly net revenue from Personal Training (in EUR).

The by far highest net revenues are realized in Switzerland with an average of 3,866 EUR per month, followed by Germany and Norway, with 2,698 and 2,618 EUR respectively. The lowest average revenue is achieved in Portugal, Austria and Finland.

Based on the individual market situations, obviously different levels of revenue are realized by Personal Trainers in the individual countries. Reasons for these differences can be, amongst others, the achievable prices in a country or the level of competition on the one hand. On the other hand, also the different shares of fulltime and parttime Personal Trainers have their impact.

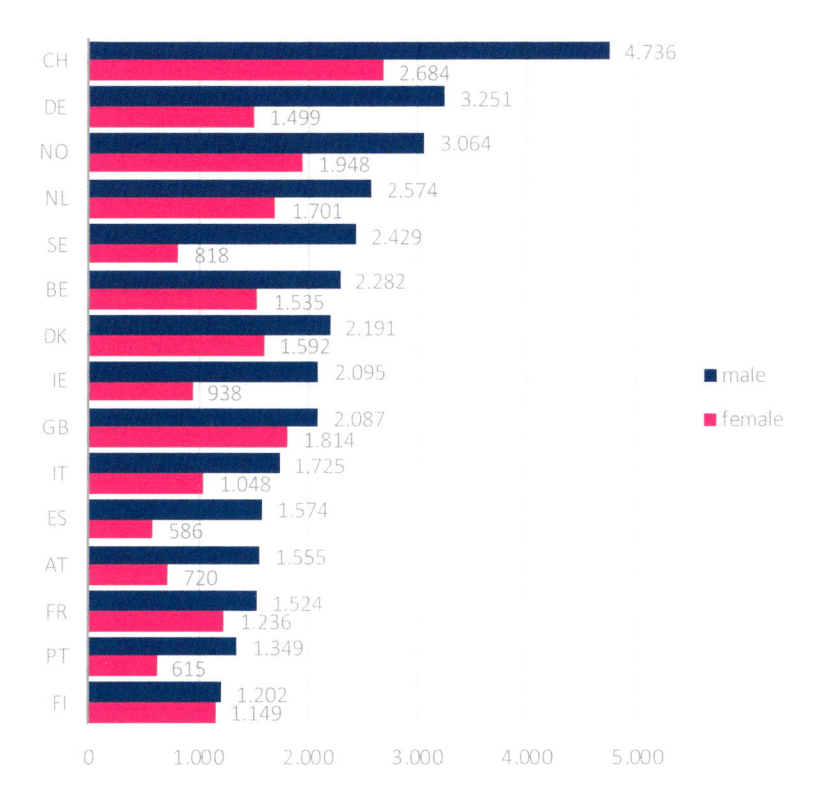

Country	Male	Female
CH	4.736	2.684
DE	3.251	1.499
NO	3.064	1.948
NL	2.574	1.701
SE	2.429	818
BE	2.282	1.535
DK	2.191	1.592
IE	2.095	938
GB	2.087	1.814
IT	1.725	1.048
ES	1.574	586
AT	1.555	720
FR	1.524	1.236
PT	1.349	615
FI	1.202	1.149

Figure 2.20: Average monthly revenue by gender (in EUR).

While male Personal Trainers achieve an average of 2,152 EUR per month in Europe, the average of female Personal Trainers is only 1,371 EUR or 781 EUR less. This picture is confirmed by the situation in the individual countries. Women do not in a single country make more money from Personal Training than men. While the largest gap of more than 2,000 EUR is seen in Switzerland it is almost on a par in Finland, the country with the strongest portion of female Personal Trainers of almost 60%.

Given the absolute numbers of revenue it is certainly interesting to see which factors influence these figures. A potential external factor is the individual local market a Personal Trainer is operating in. We have differentiated the cities where Personal Trainers work by the number of the respective inhabitants from below 25,000 to more than 1,000,000.

It is interesting to see that the level of net revenue on European average increases with the growing number of inhabitants until a city size of five million. Beyond that it is constant for the next category and even declines in cities with a population of more than one million.

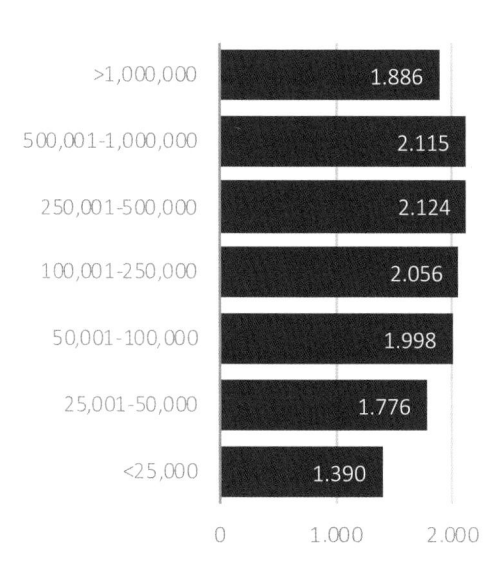

City size (inhabitants)	Average monthly net revenue (EUR)
>1,000,000	1.886
500,001-1,000,000	2.115
250,001-500,000	2.124
100,001-250,000	2.056
50,001-100,000	1.998
25,001-50,000	1.776
<25,000	1.390

Figure 2.21: Average monthly net revenue by city size (in EUR).

Besides this external parameter it might matter even more what internal factors might drive the level of income. One potential factor is the respective age of the Personal Trainer. While the level of revenue seems to be rather lower until the age of 29, it increases significantly in older age groups. While Personal Trainers in the age from 20 to 29 achieve on average 1,451 EUR all higher age groups make at least 1,930 EUR per month.

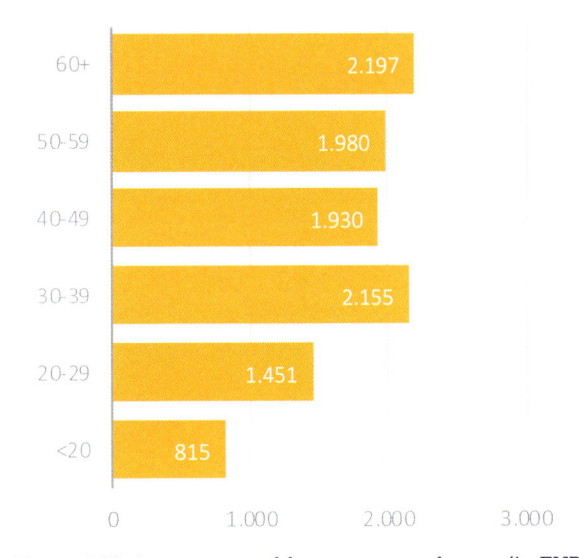

Age	Average monthly net revenue (EUR)
60+	2.197
50-59	1.980
40-49	1.930
30-39	2.155
20-29	1.451
<20	815

Figure 2.22: Average monthly net revenue by age (in EUR).

In addition to the age of a Personal Trainer also his actual time or experience as a Personal Trainer might impact his ability to realize revenue in his business. And, in fact, there seems to be a strong connection between the level of income and the time spent in this profession.

Personal Trainers with less than one year of experience make an average of 1,015 EUR per month. This amount increases with every level of experience. The group of Personal Trainers with at least 7 years of experience is able to realize 2,587 EUR per month or 2.5 times the money the new-comers achieve. So, obviously experience in his profession pays off for a Personal Trainer.

Experience (years)	Average monthly net revenue (EUR)
7+	2.587
3-6	1.768
1-2	1.238
<1	1.015

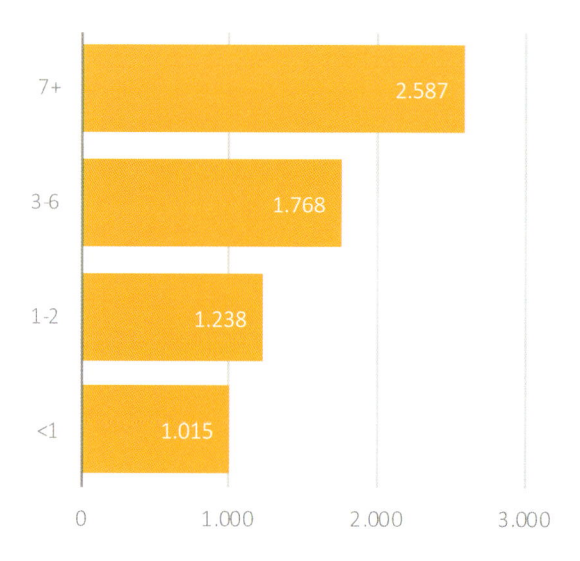

Figure 2.23: Average monthly net revenue by experience as Personal Trainer (in EUR).

Another potential influencing factor might be the individual highest level of education achieved by a Personal Trainer. And, again, there seems to be a comparable strong impact on the level of revenue. Personal Trainers with no certified fitness-related qualification or only a basic fitness-related vocational qualification both achieve an average of approximately 1,130 EUR per month.

In comparison, those Personal Trainers with a fitness-related bachelor's or even master's degree, earn an average of 2,069 EUR and 2,100 EUR respectively. Personal Trainers with a fitness-related doctorate programme achieve even higher income, however, the number of participants even at this European level is rather small and the number, therefore, of a limited reliability.

Qualification	Average monthly net revenue (EUR)
Fitness-related doctorate programme	2.923
Fitness-related graduate programme	2.100
Fitness-related bachelor's degree	2.069
Comprehensive fitness-related vocational...	2.033
Basic fitness-related vocational qualification	1.126
No certified fitness-related qualification	1.135

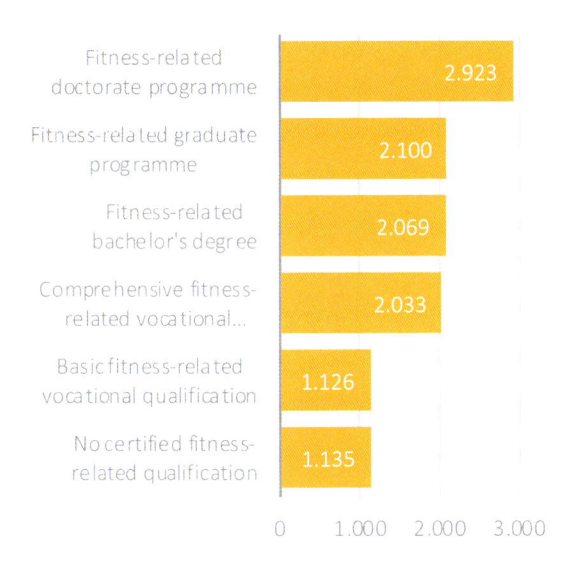

Figure 2.24: Average monthly net revenue by highest qualification (in EUR).

Still, the numbers seem to prove that the investment in respective fitness-related qualifications pays off for Personal Trainers. We will therefore also shed some light on the situation of education and qualification amongst Personal Trainers in the following.

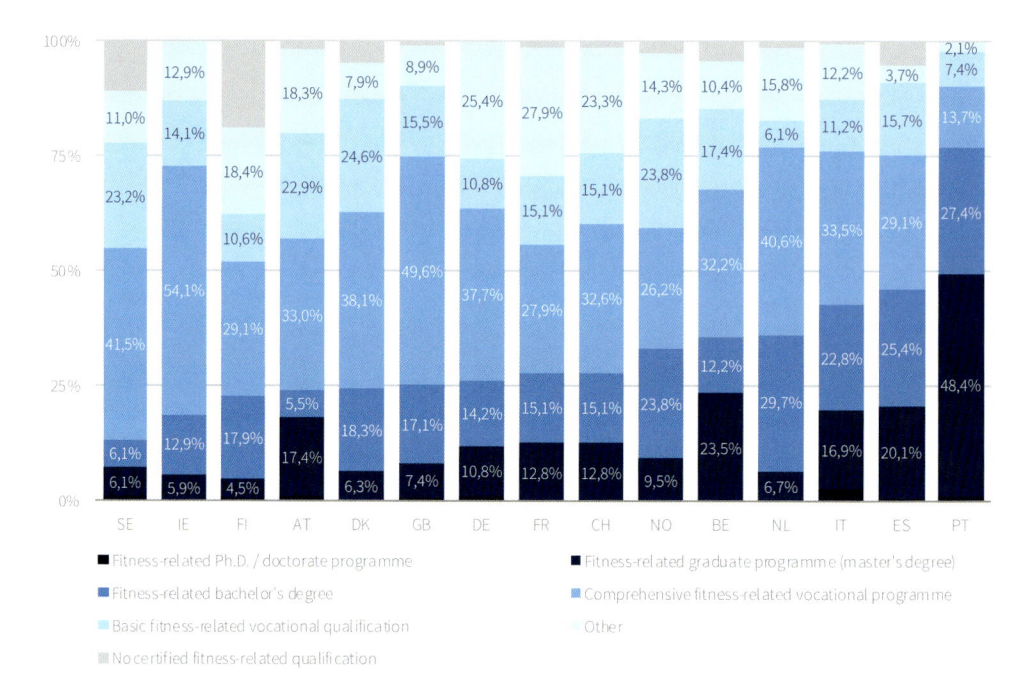

Figure 2.25: Personal Trainers' highest level of qualification.

It is generally accepted that a good education is the essential prerequisite for a successful Personal Trainer. Especially in a service-based offering like Personal Training, an adequate education is a strong selling proposition and also a requirement for customer retention.

The official educational requirements, however, differ strongly from country to country. While a Personal Trainer does not need any formal education at all to call himself a "Personal Trainer" in some countries, in others specific minimum requirements have to be fulfilled. At the same time, the educational offerings of the individual national training providers also vary greatly. Hence, the formulation of the questions in our survey, trying to cover all the different educational pathways was the subject of a lively discussion.

When looking at the highest level of education achieved by the participating Personal Trainers, it becomes evident that comprehensive fitness-related vocational programmes are the most commonly provided educational level in most of the countries. Their share ranges from 26.2% in Norway to 54.1% in Ireland; only in Portugal is their proportion significantly lower, with 13.6%. In Portugal, the highest share of Personal Trainers (48.4%) actually have fitness-related graduate programmes with a master's degree. It is by far the highest portion of this comparably high level of education followed by Belgium and Austria.

The difficulty in covering and comparing the individual education approaches, again, becomes apparent in the high portion of other levels of education that have been stated by the participants. In France, for instance, 27.9% of the participating Personal Trainers stated that they have achieved an educational level not covered by the defined ones.

Even though the analysis unveils a highly heterogeneous and opaque landscape of educational offerings in the different countries, it also shows that only a very limited number of Personal Trainers has no certified fitness-related qualification. Only Sweden and

Finland have a higher portion of these non-qualified trainers, although, the significant deviation in these two countries from the others could also arise from translation issues.

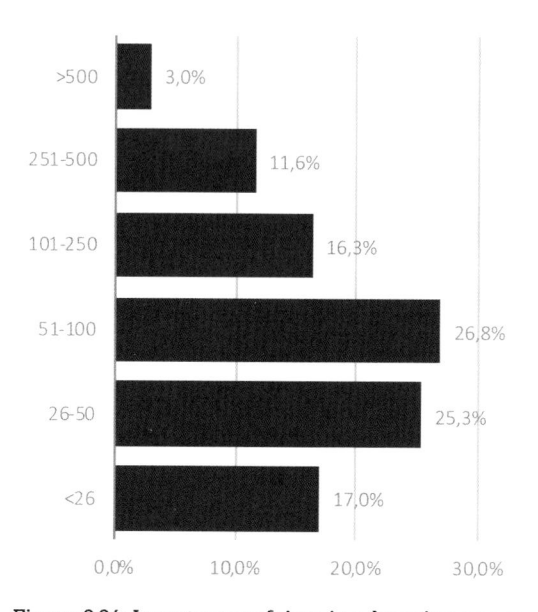

Hours	Percentage
>500	3,0%
251-500	11,6%
101-250	16,3%
51-100	26,8%
26-50	25,3%
<26	17,0%

Figure 2.26: Investment of time in education per year (hours).

Given the importance of qualification as shown before, it is interesting to see how much time and money Personal Trainers actually invest in their profession. More than half of the participating Personal Trainers state to invest between 26 and 100 hours per year into on-going education. Only 17% devote less than that. Almost one third of these Personal Trainers claim to invest more than 100 hours per year.

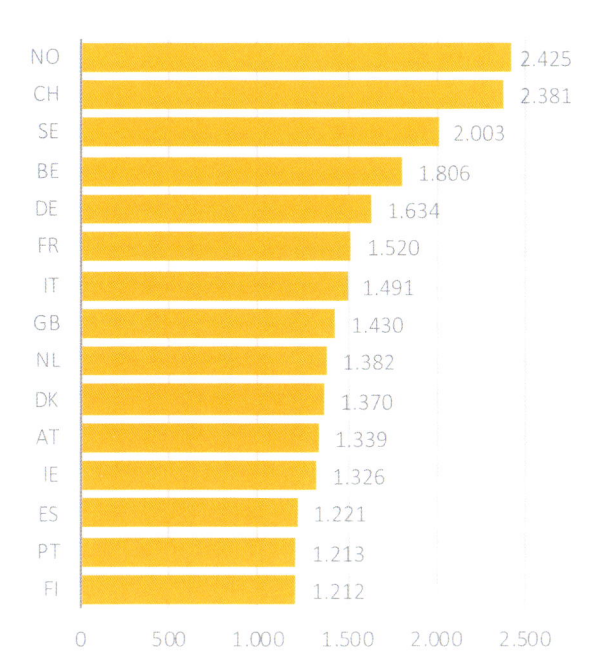

Country	EUR
NO	2.425
CH	2.381
SE	2.003
BE	1.806
DE	1.634
FR	1.520
IT	1.491
GB	1.430
NL	1.382
DK	1.370
AT	1.339
IE	1.326
ES	1.221
PT	1.213
FI	1.212

Figure 2.27: Investment of money in education per year (EUR).

With respect to the money invested in education the amounts vary significantly between the individual countries. While Personal Trainers in Norway and Switzerland spend on average approximately 2,400 EUR per year, those in Spain, Portugal as well as Finland only invest about 1,200 EUR or half the money of their colleagues.

Knowing how much Personal Trainers invest in their qualification, it is the obvious next question which areas are the decisive ones. When asked what the important skills for Personal Trainers are, 85.7% of the participants answered personality skills followed by the willingness to learn and customer service skills. The hard facts, namely specific technical skills are ranked only sixth. IT or digital skills are rated the least important and by only 13.9% of the respondents as very important.

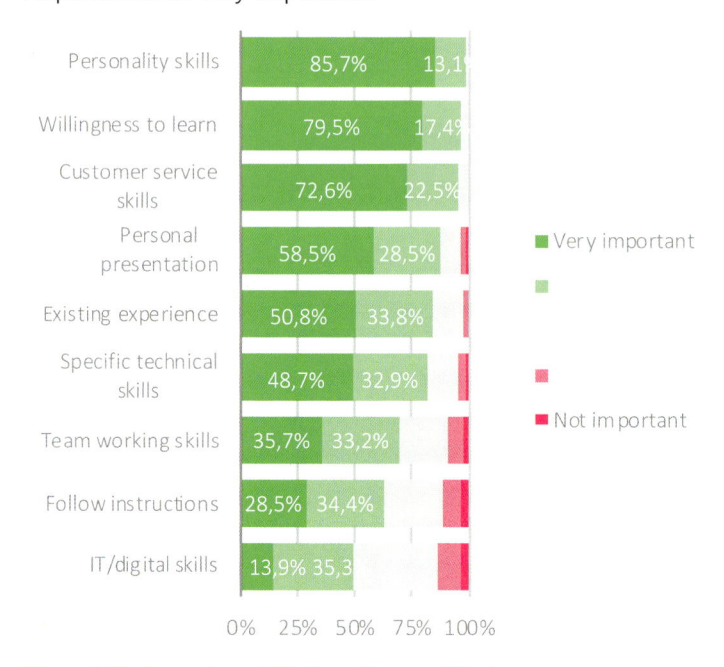

Skill	Very important	(middle)	Not important
Personality skills	85,7%	13,1%	
Willingness to learn	79,5%	17,4%	
Customer service skills	72,6%	22,5%	
Personal presentation	58,5%	28,5%	
Existing experience	50,8%	33,8%	
Specific technical skills	48,7%	32,9%	
Team working skills	35,7%	33,2%	
Follow instructions	28,5%	34,4%	
IT/digital skills	13,9%	35,3%	

Figure 2.28: Important skills for a Personal Trainer.

Against the background of this somewhat complex and opaque international educational system in the fitness industry, a majority of Personal Trainers assesses international standards as useful. The strongest consent is seen in Ireland, Finland, and Belgium, whereas the United Kingdom, Spain, and especially Sweden show the lowest agreement. Only 18.5% of the participants in Sweden see international standards as very useful compared to 54.8% in Ireland.

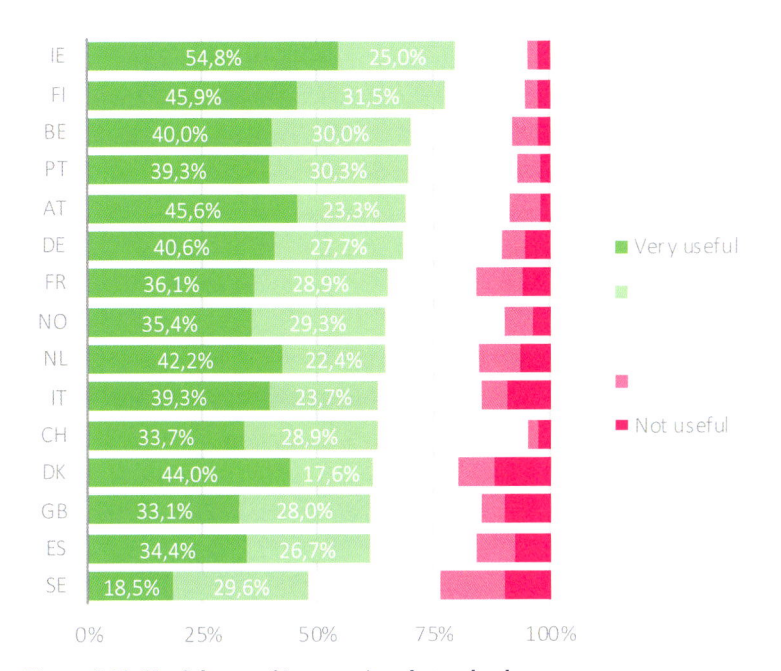

	Very useful		Not useful
IE	54,8%	25,0%	
FI	45,9%	31,5%	
BE	40,0%	30,0%	
PT	39,3%	30,3%	
AT	45,6%	23,3%	
DE	40,6%	27,7%	
FR	36,1%	28,9%	
NO	35,4%	29,3%	
NL	42,2%	22,4%	
IT	39,3%	23,7%	
CH	33,7%	28,9%	
DK	44,0%	17,6%	
GB	33,1%	28,0%	
ES	34,4%	26,7%	
SE	18,5%	29,6%	

Figure 2.29: Usefulness of international standards.

However, the vast majority of Personal Trainers has a positive understanding of international standardisation. On a pan-European basis two-thirds of the Personal Trainers state that such standards would be useful or even very useful and only 12% worry about a negative influence.

One driving force for the development of international standards, not only for Personal Trainers but fitness professionals in general, is the European Register of Exercise Professionals (EREPS) as part of the European health and fitness association, EuropeActive. A key prerequisite in influencing the international situation is the awareness in the different countries and amongst the individual trainers of EREPS. Based on our survey, we have determined significant variances in the awareness of EREPS between the different countries.

In Finland, almost three-quarters of the participating Personal Trainers know about EREPS; in Denmark it is more than two thirds. In contrast, in Switzerland only 11.8% and in Austria even as little as 7.8% are aware of EREPS. Interestingly, 68.9% of the participants in Austria at the same time think that international standards would be helpful for Personal Trainers. Obviously, there seems to be some growth potential for EREPS's awareness together with the development of international standards in selected European countries.

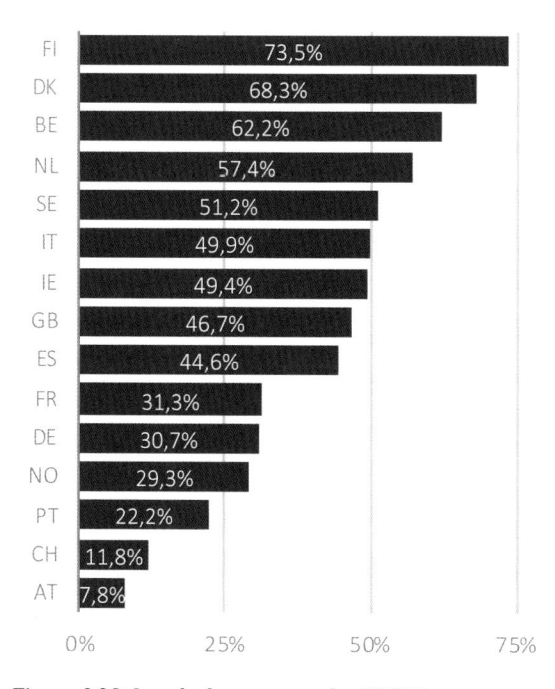

Country	Awareness
FI	73,5%
DK	68,3%
BE	62,2%
NL	57,4%
SE	51,2%
IT	49,9%
IE	49,4%
GB	46,7%
ES	44,6%
FR	31,3%
DE	30,7%
NO	29,3%
PT	22,2%
CH	11,8%
AT	7,8%

Figure 2.30: Level of awareness for EREPS.

2.4 Offering and Prices

In this section, the offerings and prices of Personal Training will be presented, including types and locations, and prices per session.

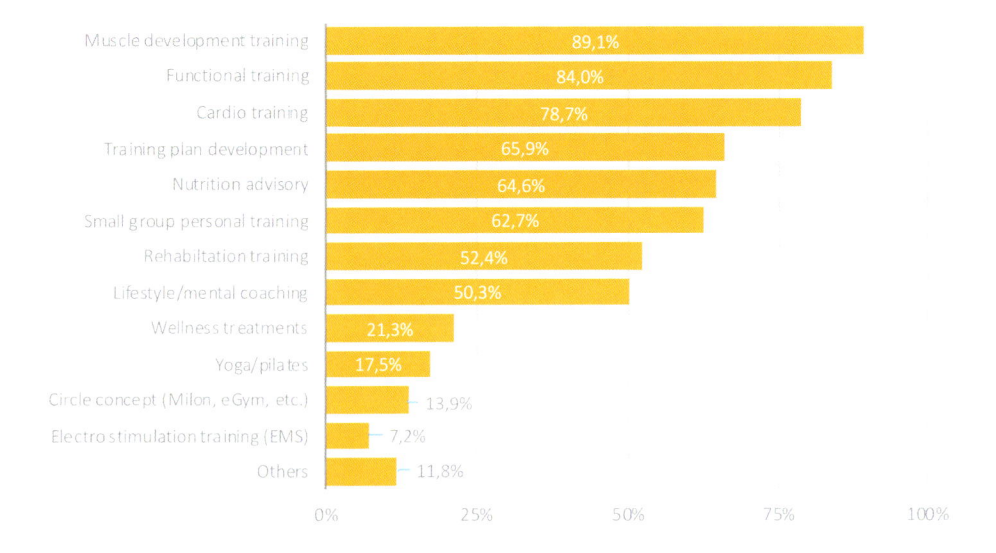

Service	Percentage
Muscle development training	89,1%
Functional training	84,0%
Cardio training	78,7%
Training plan development	65,9%
Nutrition advisory	64,6%
Small group personal training	62,7%
Rehabilitation training	52,4%
Lifestyle/mental coaching	50,3%
Wellness treatments	21,3%
Yoga/pilates	17,5%
Circle concept (Milon, eGym, etc.)	13,9%
Electro stimulation training (EMS)	7,2%
Others	11,8%

Figure 2.31: Services of within Personal Training.

Another area of interest is the actual offering of Personal Trainers. With respect to these services, three different offerings stand out: 89.1% of the participating trainers offer muscle development training and 78.7% cardio training, which can obviously be seen as the core services of a Personal Trainer.

It is interesting to see that 84.0% of the trainers apply and offer functional fitness methods in their work. A second group of services is offered by two-thirds to half of the Personal Trainers. Amongst these are training plan development, nutrition advisory as well as lifestyle or mental coaching.

As of now, services like wellness treatments, yoga or pilates, circle concepts as well as electro stimulation training play a rather subordinate role in the offering of Personal Trainers.

Given the individual services, we also asked the trainers about the amount of different organisational forms of training they delivered. In this regard, besides the actual session with one client we also asked about training with two clients at the same time and training with a small group.

As expected, the "traditional" 1-on-1 training has the greatest importance in the work of Personal Trainers. Based on our survey, 72.4% of the training is realised in this format. The second most important format is small group training with 17.3%, while 1-on-2 makes 10.3% of the overall Personal Training sessions.

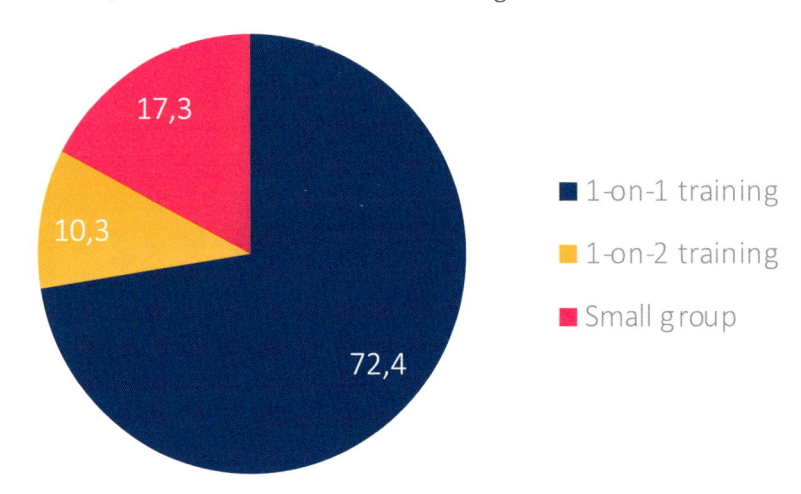

Figure 2.32: Types of offering.

In search for a definition of small group in this context, we asked what the specific maximum number of participants in such a training session is for the Personal Trainers. 42.7% indicate two to four participants and 27.0% state five to seven within one group. The number of eight to ten participants is considered by 17.8% and 12.4% finally think that more than ten people could be coached within a small group. Therefore, 70% of the Personal Trainers define a small group as a group of seven or less.

As the understanding of a small group differs between the Personal Trainers, the importance of the respective forms of organisation also varies not only on the individual but also on the national level. Portugal and Norway seem to have a rather "classic" Personal Training offering with a share of 85.3% and 84.3% of 1-on-1 training. In comparison, in Austria and Ireland the 1-on-1 share is around 60% and small group training has a portion of 20% to even 30%. While the portion of 1-on-2 training varies only by 4.6 percentage points, the share of small group training differs by more than 20 percentage points between the individual countries. It will be interesting to see in future research, how this distribution of the individual organisational forms might change.

Country	1-on-1 training	1-on-2 training	Small group
PT	85,3	7,5	7,2
NO	84,3	7,4	8,3
CH	78,7	5,1	16,2
GB	78,7	9,8	11,6
DK	75,9	9,0	15,1
DE	75,1	9,1	15,7
BE	74,1	11,4	14,5
FI	73,6	7,0	19,4
SE	70,9	8,9	20,2
IT	70,4	10,9	18,6
NL	68,9	11,0	20,0
ES	68,5	12,6	19,0
FR	66,0	11,5	22,5
IE	63,1	13,6	23,3
AT	59,7	12,1	28,2

Figure 2.33: Types of offering by country.

Another question when thinking of the offering of a Personal Trainer is "where" the trainer offers his services. Based on our survey, three different types of locations are obviously the most commonly used. For the employed trainers the employers' health and fitness club is the location used the most, while this is the club of a cooperation partner for the self-employed trainers. Own facilities are used by 49.0% of the participating trainers.

Almost one quarter of the Personal Training sessions of our participants are realised outdoors. 22.1% of the sessions take place at the client's home. Other locations of the client such as his fitness club or his work place are used in only 17.1% or 7.9% of the sessions, respectively. It seems to be the prevailing case that the client has to get to the trainer more often than the other way around.

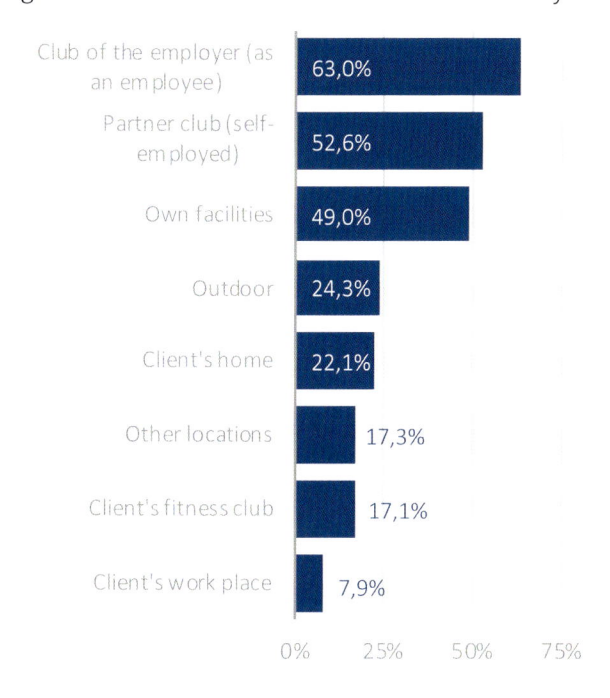

Location	Percentage
Club of the employer (as an employee)	63,0%
Partner club (self-employed)	52,6%
Own facilities	49,0%
Outdoor	24,3%
Client's home	22,1%
Other locations	17,3%
Client's fitness club	17,1%
Client's work place	7,9%

Figure 2.34: Location of offering.

Against the background of the individual services offered by Personal Trainers and their respective organisational form, it is the obvious next question to ask what clients have to pay for these services.

Based on our research, the average price for a 1-on-1 session is 53 EUR. The price female Personal Trainers charge is higher than the price of their male colleagues. While women on average charge 60 EUR, it is 50 EUR when the trainers are men. This would seem a surprising result, given the gender wage gap which in many countries still exists. To some extent it could be explained by the large number of male Personal Trainers in countries with comparably lower price levels such as Italy and Spain.

However, these prices at the individual national levels are also of a higher validity than the general average over 15 countries with different market situations, price levels and so on.

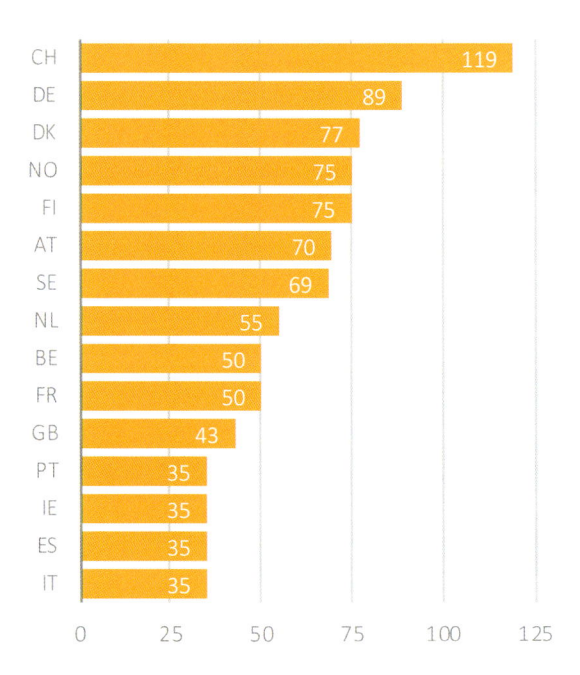

Country	Price (EUR)
CH	119
DE	89
DK	77
NO	75
FI	75
AT	70
SE	69
NL	55
BE	50
FR	50
GB	43
PT	35
IE	35
ES	35
IT	35

Figure 2.35: Prices per session (in EUR).

As already indicated, the prices for a Personal Training session seem to be the lowest in the three South-European countries Italy, Spain, and Portugal together with Ireland. In all four countries the average price is 35 EUR. The Personal Training market in the United Kingdom seems to be at a similar level as the Irish market with an average of 43 EUR.

At a higher level but also comparable amongst each other are the prices in Belgium, the Netherlands, and France between 50 and 55 EUR. The Scandinavian group including Sweden, Finland, Norway, and Denmark shows a rather homogeneous pricing standard between 69 and 77 EUR.

By far the highest average price for a 1-on-1 session is realised in Switzerland with 119 EUR. This is 30 EUR or 25% higher than in the second most expensive market Germany, where the average session costs 89 EUR.

Note: All prices mentioned in this section are including VAT.

Country	1-on-1	1-on-2	Small group
CH	119	92	37
DE	89	60	30
DK	77	60	40
NO	75	65	40
FI	75	60	35
AT	70	50	15
SE	69	53	40
NL	55	35	20
FR	50	35	20
BE	50	30	15
GB	43	31	18
IT	35	25	15
ES	35	25	19
IE	35	25	16
PT	35	25	19

Table 2.3: Prices per session (in EUR).

Besides the pricing for the traditional Personal Training session with one client at a time, the prices for complementary offerings such as 1-on-2 and small group training are also of interest. While the international average price for the 1-on-1 session is 53 EUR, it is 40 EUR per person in the 1-on-2 and 20 EUR in a small group environment. Unsurprisingly, on a national level the distribution of prices in the two other categories is very similar to the one in 1-on-1 training.

Beyond the description of the actual prices of Personal Training in the individual markets, the relation of the prices to specific parameters might be worth examining.

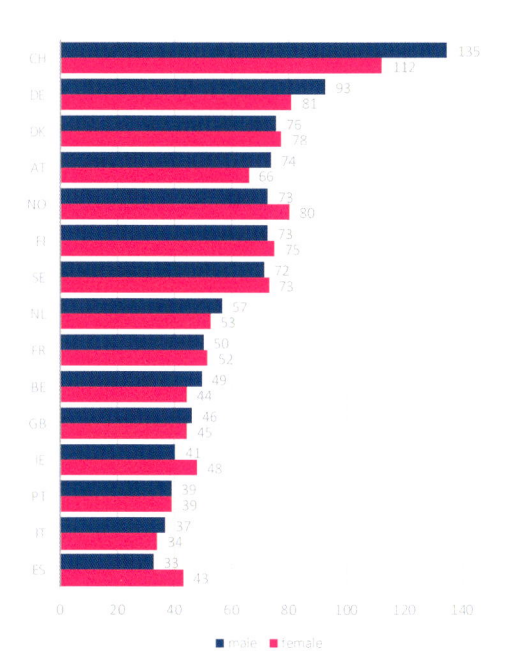

Figure 2.36: Relation of price to gender (in EUR).

In contrast to the overall achieved revenue, female Personal Trainers seem to be able to achieve higher prices for their individual Personal Training sessions compared to their male colleagues. While the average price for a Personal Training session with a male trainer is 57.50 EUR, female trainers charge on average 63.10 EUR. A gap of 5.60 EUR or almost 10%.

With respect to the individual countries, we have identified eight countries where prices for female Personal Trainers are higher compared to male trainers. The biggest price difference in favour of female Personal Trainers is seen in Spain (10.40 EUR) and Ireland (7.50 EUR). In contrast, male Personal Trainers in Switzerland charge on average 22.30 EUR more than female trainers. The contrast between the higher prices and lower revenue might to some extent be explained by the higher portion of female parttime Personal Trainers.

As already seen with respect to revenue from Personal Training, a relation between prices for Personal Training and different internal as well as external factors can also be identified.

Figure 2.37: Relation of price to education.

Qualification	Price per 1-on-1 training session
Fitness-related doctorate programme	68,6
Fitness-related graduate programme	57,5
Fitness-related bachelor's degree	57,7
Comprehensive fitness-related vocational programme	58,1
Basic fitness-related vocational qualification	53,3

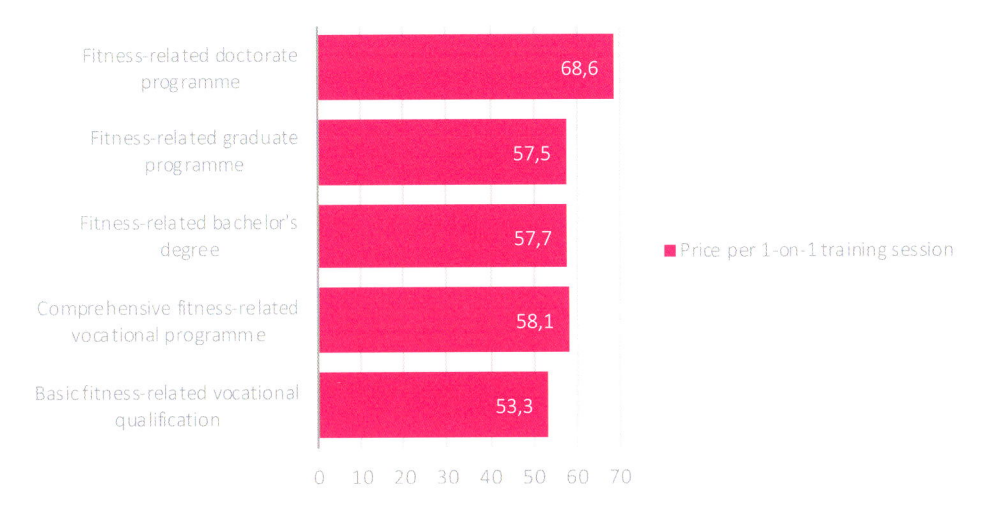

Figure 2.37: Relation of price to education.

The highest fitness-related qualification achieved by a Personal Trainer seems to have a positive impact on the price to be charged by Personal Trainers. While Personal Trainers with a basic qualification charge 53.30 EUR the price increases with higher levels of education.

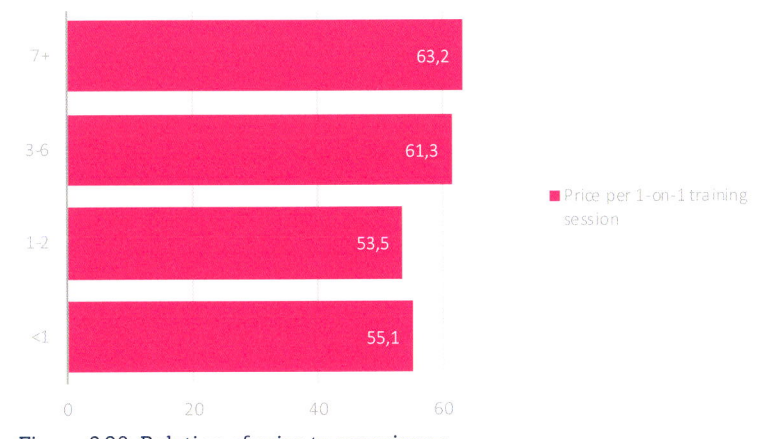

Years of experience	Price per 1-on-1 training session
7+	63,2
3-6	61,3
1-2	53,5
<1	55,1

Figure 2.38: Relation of price to experience.

Also, the respective experience as well the external factor of the size of the city a Personal Trainer is working in has an impact on the price of Personal Training session.

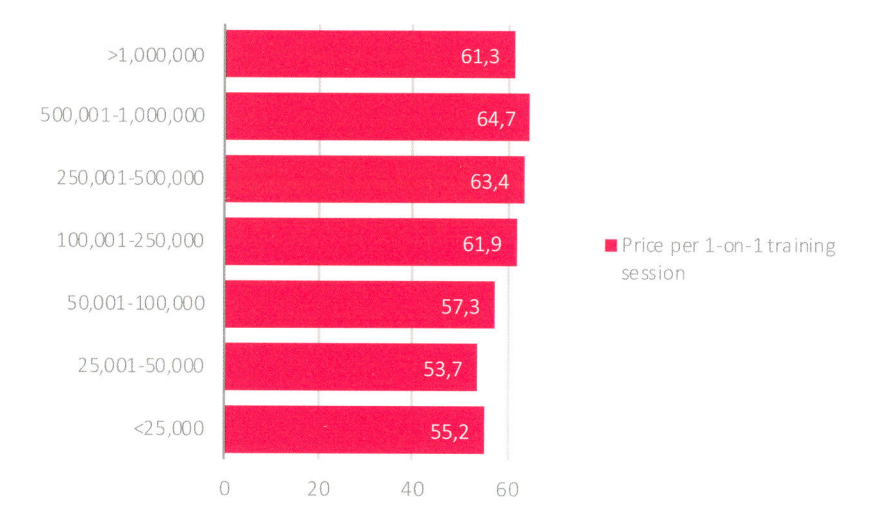

City size	Price per 1-on-1 training session
>1,000,000	61,3
500,001-1,000,000	64,7
250,001-500,000	63,4
100,001-250,000	61,9
50,001-100,000	57,3
25,001-50,000	53,7
<25,000	55,2

Figure 2.39: Relation of price to city size.

The development and growing importance of technology is a key driver in many industries. We, therefore, also asked the Personal Trainers in our survey for their usage and expectations of technology in general and also about specific use cases.

The most used piece of technology amongst Personal Trainers is the smartphone. 72.2% of the participants state that they generally use their phone for work. In comparison, computers and laptops are used by only 61.6% today. Other more often used technical aids are timers, tablets, and wearables. The "traditional" telephone, connected gym equipment as well as video telephony are used only by a minority of Personal Trainers.

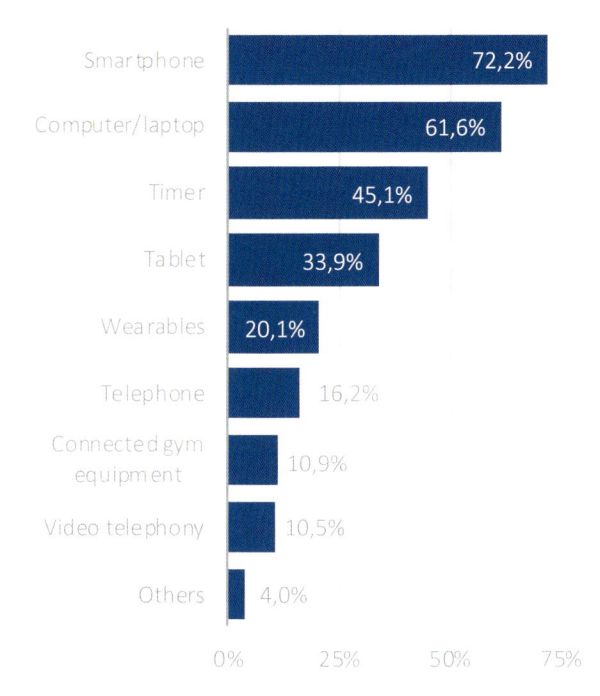

Technology	Percentage
Smartphone	72,2%
Computer/laptop	61,6%
Timer	45,1%
Tablet	33,9%
Wearables	20,1%
Telephone	16,2%
Connected gym equipment	10,9%
Video telephony	10,5%
Others	4,0%

Figure 2.40: Use of Technology (general).

With respect to the measurement and tracking of their clients' development, most Personal Trainers take digital notes (59.3%) as well as the "old-school" notes with pen and paper (54.6%). All other forms of tracking are used only by a smaller number of trainers. Wearables, for instance, are used by 16.2% of the participating trainers in their Personal Training work.

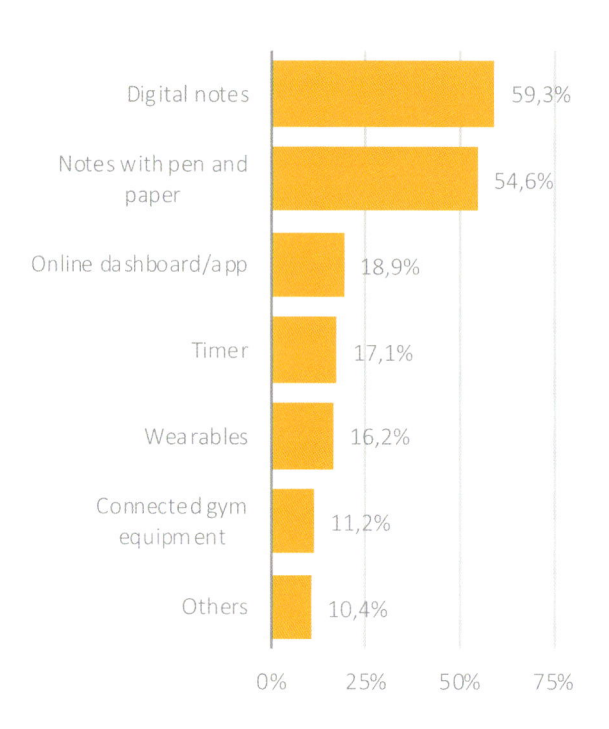

Figure 2.41: Use of Technology (tracking).

Asked for their clients' preferred tracking methods, again digital (51.6%) as well as pen and paper notes (50.2%) are by far the most relevant types. However, online dashboard/apps (42.1%) and also wearables (35.6%) do play a significantly higher role for clients compared to their trainers.

Also, for the submission of training plans to their clients, Personal Trainers predominantly use digital as well as pen and paper notes.

Furthermore, 34.9% of Personal Trainers only communicate training plans personally to their clients.

Method	Percentage
Digital notes	64,1%
Notes with pen and paper	43,7%
Only personally	34,9%
Online dashboard/app	17,6%
Only remotely & verbal	6,2%
Others	4,1%

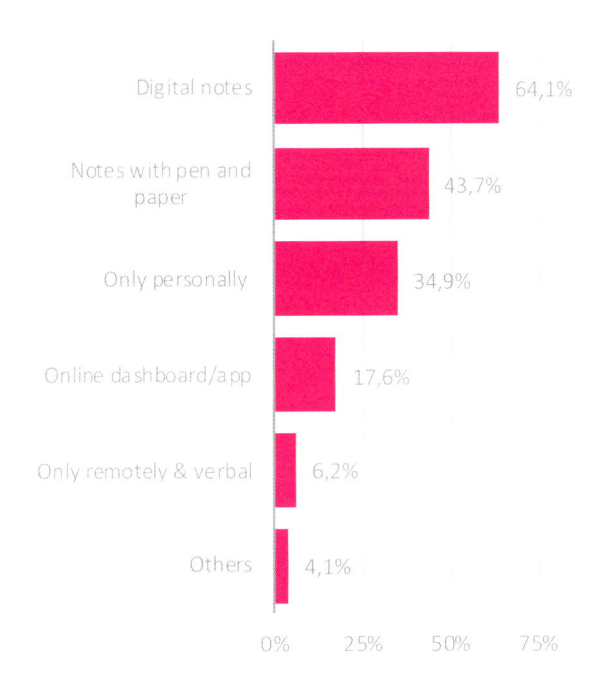

Figure 2.42: Use of Technology (training plan).

With regard to their expectations for the future importance of technology in their field, the vast majority of Personal Trainer sees an increasing usage. In all the countries under investigation at least 82.7% (France) of the respondents expect at least an increase of technology usage in their work. In France, at the same time, also the highest portion of trainers expect a decrease in the usage; however, this portion with 5.2% is relatively small. The strongest belief in an increasing usage is amongst the Personal Trainers in Spain and Portugal. 97.6% of the Spanish participants expect an increase or even a strong increase in the importance of technology for Personal Trainers.

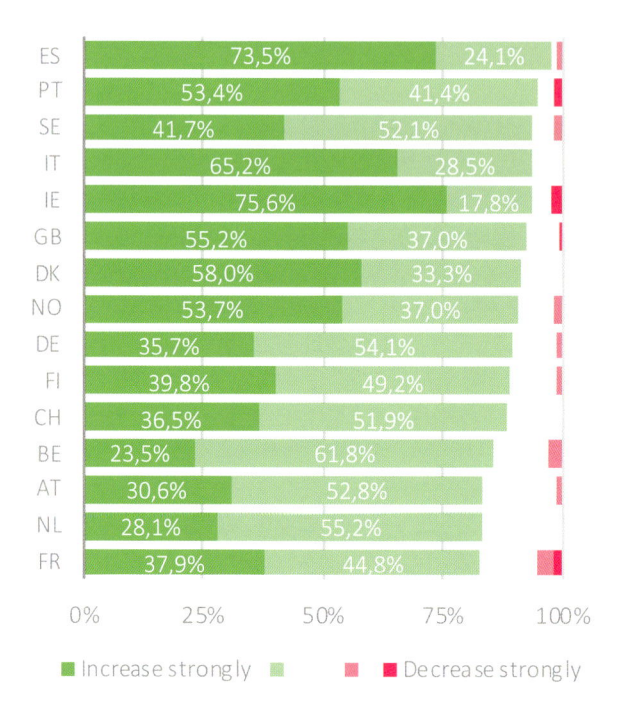

Country	Increase strongly	Increase	Decrease	Decrease strongly
ES	73,5%	24,1%		
PT	53,4%	41,4%		
SE	41,7%	52,1%		
IT	65,2%	28,5%		
IE	75,6%	17,8%		
GB	55,2%	37,0%		
DK	58,0%	33,3%		
NO	53,7%	37,0%		
DE	35,7%	54,1%		
FI	39,8%	49,2%		
CH	36,5%	51,9%		
BE	23,5%	61,8%		
AT	30,6%	52,8%		
NL	28,1%	55,2%		
FR	37,9%	44,8%		

Figure 2.43: Development of usage of technology.

A similar picture is seen with regard to the willingness to use wearable technology to support fitness training. Again, the highest willingness can be seen amongst the Personal Trainers in Spain and Portugal. However, the share is lower compared to the general expectations of technology. 79.5% of the participants in Spain agree or completely agree with the statement that they would like to use (more) wearable technology. In the second placed country Portugal 72.4% share the same assessment. The other countries are significantly behind this figure.

The "weakest" markets for wearable technology seem to be Switzerland, Sweden, Germany, and Austria where only 30% to 40% agree with the statement concerning the potential usage of wearables.

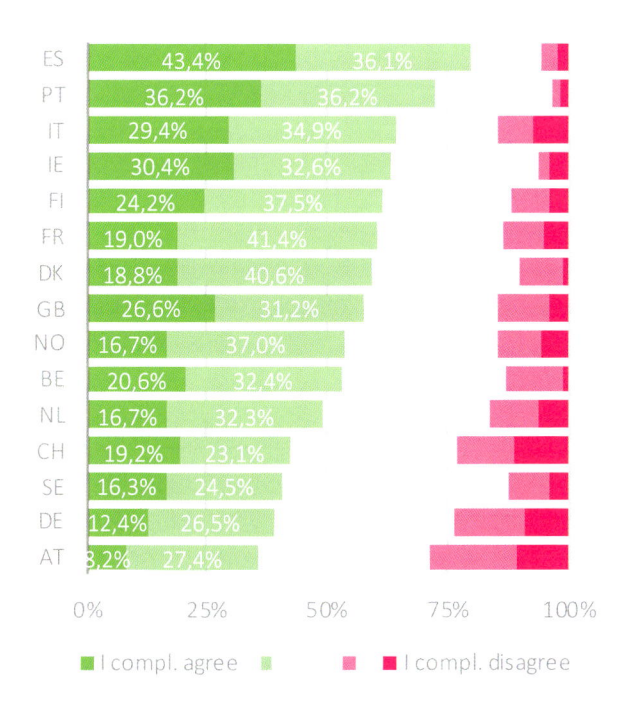

Country	I compl. agree	agree
ES	43,4%	36,1%
PT	36,2%	36,2%
IT	29,4%	34,9%
IE	30,4%	32,6%
FI	24,2%	37,5%
FR	19,0%	41,4%
DK	18,8%	40,6%
GB	26,6%	31,2%
NO	16,7%	37,0%
BE	20,6%	32,4%
NL	16,7%	32,3%
CH	19,2%	23,1%
SE	16,3%	24,5%
DE	12,4%	26,5%
AT	8,2%	27,4%

Figure 2.44: Willingness to use wearables.

In addition to the query of sheer numbers, we included an unaided question about relevant technology brands. Personal Trainers by far most often named Polar as the brand for wearables with a leading edge. Other companies mentioned are Fitbit, Garmin, Apple, Suunto, TomTom, and Nike. Amongst the brands related to connected gym equipment, Personal Trainers particularly named Technogym and, again, Polar followed by Life Fitness and egym.

2.5 Clients and Marketing

One of the obviously most interesting aspects in the field of Personal Training is the clients themselves. We have, therefore, integrated questions related to the clients of the Personal Trainers into our survey. However, as we have conducted a survey only amongst the trainers within our research, we could only rely on this indirect assessment of the clients, here. It would be the purpose of a survey amongst Personal Training clients to achieve even more detailed information in this area.

Based on our survey, the majority of Personal Training clients are women. On international average, almost two-thirds (64.7%) of all clients are female. This picture is confirmed when looking into the individual countries. In all the different markets women account for at least 58.9% of the Personal Training clients.

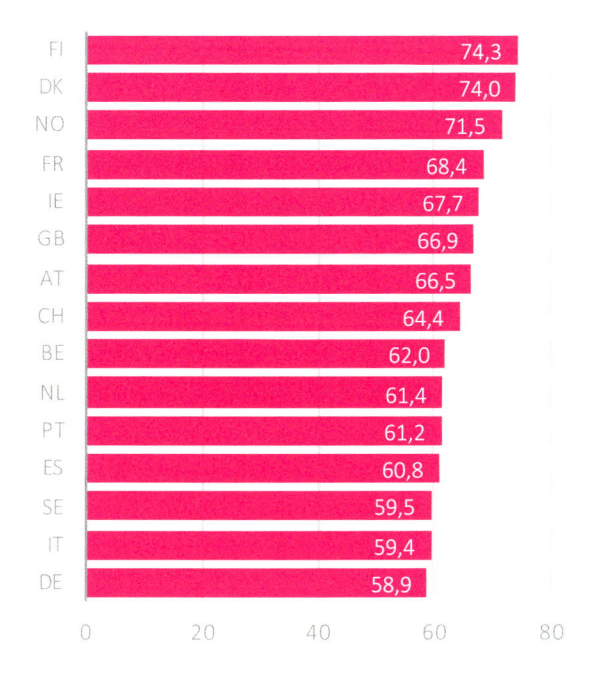

Country	%
FI	74,3
DK	74,0
NO	71,5
FR	68,4
IE	67,7
GB	66,9
AT	66,5
CH	64,4
BE	62,0
NL	61,4
PT	61,2
ES	60,8
SE	59,5
IT	59,4
DE	58,9

Figure 2.45: Portion of female clients (in %).

The lowest share of women is seen in Germany, Italy, and Sweden. In contrast to Sweden, the three other Scandinavian countries are those with the highest share of female clients. In Finland and Denmark almost three-quarters of Personal Training clients are women.

Another relevant parameter in the categorisation of clients is their age. When looking at the distribution of clients into different age groups, it becomes evident that more than half of the clients are in the group of the 30- to-49-year-old. The age groups 30 to 39 and 40 to 49 are relatively equally distributed. While it might be less surprising that clients of an age below 30 do not play a major role in the Personal Training, it is to some extent surprising that people of 60 years and older only account for 6.6%.

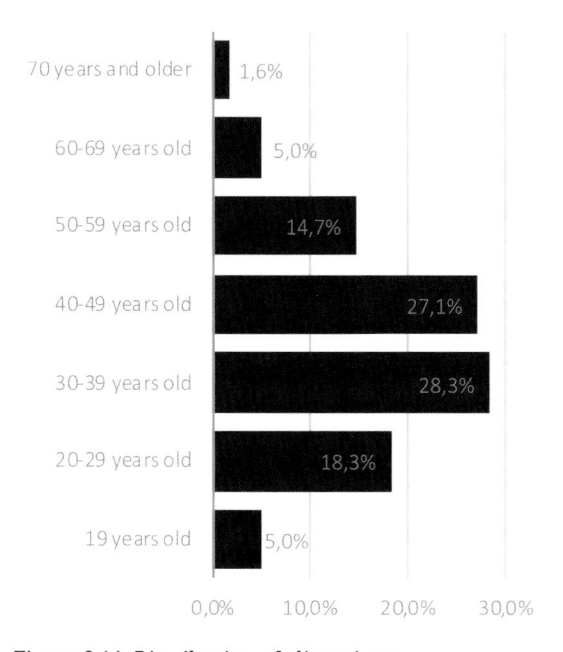

Age group	Percentage
70 years and older	1,6%
60-69 years old	5,0%
50-59 years old	14,7%
40-49 years old	27,1%
30-39 years old	28,3%
20-29 years old	18,3%
19 years old	5,0%

Figure 2.46: Distribution of clients' age.

The often-proclaimed trend towards the older customer groups and their market power does not seem to have affected the Personal Training market significantly so far. In the group of the so-called "best-agers", at least the 50-to-59-year-olds are represented fairly with a share of 14.7%.

When comparing the average age between the different markets, it varies between 36 and 42 years. The "youngest" Personal Training clients are seen in Ireland and the United Kingdom; the oldest in Portugal and Germany.

A third sociodemographic parameter is the clients' employment situation. In this respect, half of the clients or exactly 50.5% are employed. The second largest group are the self-employed clients who account for 24.7% of Personal Training clients. All other groups comprise less than 10% of all clients, namely students 7.8%, house husbands/ housewives 6.8%, and pensioners 5.3%. Professional athletes only account for 2.8% of the total number of clients.

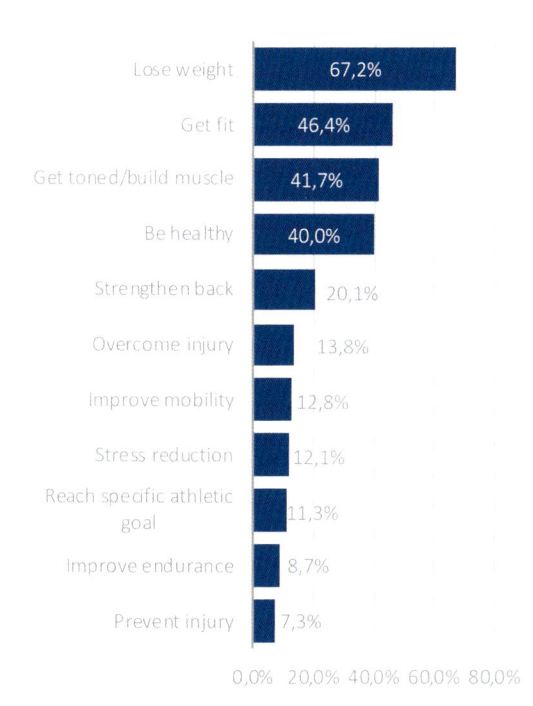

Goal	Percentage
Lose weight	67,2%
Get fit	46,4%
Get toned/build muscle	41,7%
Be healthy	40,0%
Strengthen back	20,1%
Overcome injury	13,8%
Improve mobility	12,8%
Stress reduction	12,1%
Reach specific athletic goal	11,3%
Improve endurance	8,7%
Prevent injury	7,3%

Figure 2.47: Goal of clients.

Beyond the purely sociodemographic description of the client base, it is important to understand the respective goals of clients, that is, the aim they want to reach with a Personal Trainer. By far the most important goal in Personal Training is weight loss. Two-thirds of the trainers see to lose weight as the most important aim of their clients. It is followed by get fit, get toned/build muscle and be healthy, which all comprise 40.0% to 46.2%. Besides strengthen back, which is seen as an important goal of 20.1% of the clients, all other goals account for a maximum of 13.8% of clients.

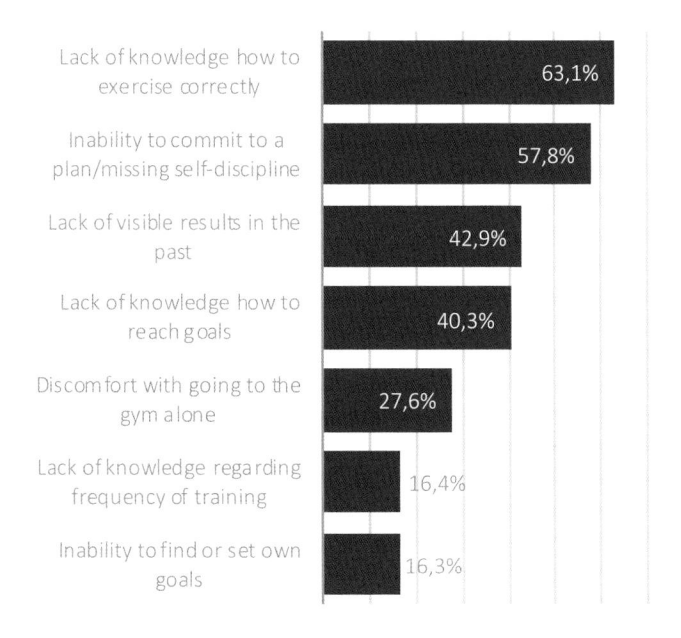

Reason	Percentage
Lack of knowledge how to exercise correctly	63,1%
Inability to commit to a plan/missing self-discipline	57,8%
Lack of visible results in the past	42,9%
Lack of knowledge how to reach goals	40,3%
Discomfort with going to the gym alone	27,6%
Lack of knowledge regarding frequency of training	16,4%
Inability to find or set own goals	16,3%

Figure 2.48: Reasons for Personal Training.

Besides the basic underlying goal which is desired to be reached with the training, we have also asked what is seen as the specific reason to choose a Personal Trainer. The most frequent reason relates to a lack of knowledge about how to exercise correctly (63.1%). The second most frequent answer is the inability to commit to a plan or missing self-discipline (57.8%) both of which have their roots in the motivation of the client.

A lack of visible results in the past is seen as the third most important reason (42.9%) by the Personal Trainers. Besides the absence of results from the clients' previous training efforts on their own, the social reason discomfort with going to the gym alone is seen as another major reason to choose a Personal Trainer.

Another view on Personal Training clients is the operational perspective of the trainers. Therefore, we have asked the participants how many clients they have in total in their client base as well as how many individual clients they have per month on average.

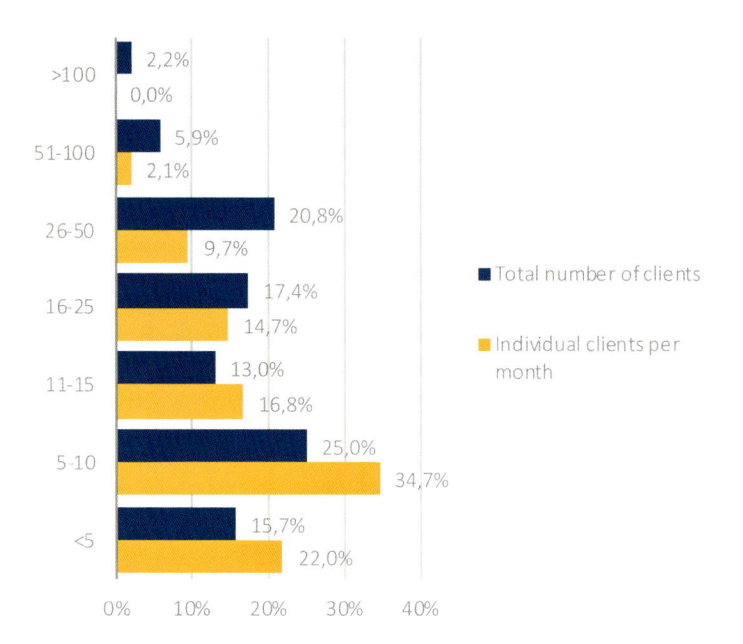

Figure 2.49: Number of clients.

With respect to the total number of clients the majority (71.1%) of Personal Trainers have a maximum of 25 clients. This includes 40.7% supporting one to ten clients in total. 20.6% respondents work with 26 to 50 clients and only 8.1% trainers state that they have more than 50 clients. A different picture is seen in the average number of individual clients per month. 56.7% work with one to ten different clients per month. Another 31.5% serve eleven to 25 clients. More than 25 clients per month is realised by 11.8%, only. It becomes obvious that the number of clients per Personal Trainer is mostly limited to a base of approximately 25 clients. In contrast, the number of Personal Trainers with a client base of more than 50 clients is very limited.

In order to achieve an even more detailed picture of the training behaviour of Personal Training clients, we have also asked the Personal Trainers about the average frequency of training sessions with their clients. The most prevalent number of training sessions is one to three times a week. 73.5% of clients' exercise in that rhythm. Only 2.9% choose a higher training frequency. On the other side of the spectrum, regular visits two to three times a month are realized by 11.5% and only once per month or less by 7.0% of clients. It is an interesting information that not more than 5.2% book a session with a Personal Trainer only once. Obviously, Personal Trainers are mostly able to convince their customers to continue their joint work after an initial trial session.

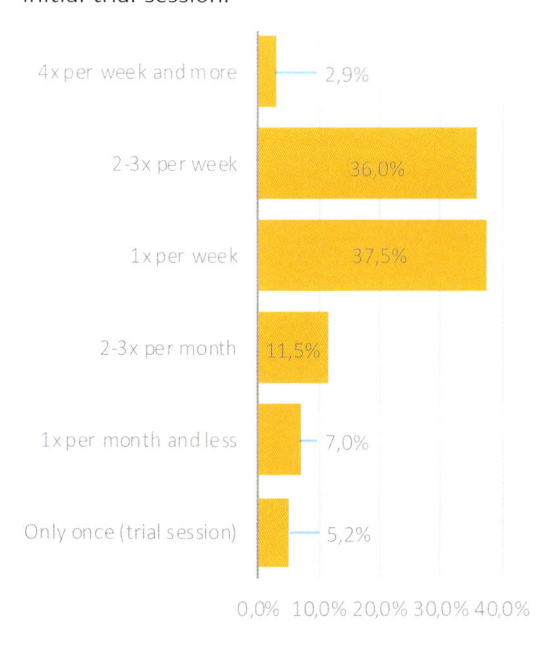

Frequency	Percentage
4x per week and more	2,9%
2-3x per week	36,0%
1x per week	37,5%
2-3x per month	11,5%
1x per month and less	7,0%
Only once (trial session)	5,2%

Figure 2.50: Frequency of clients' visits.

As in other segments of the health and fitness industry, the perception and importance of retention is growing in the Personal Training segment. Especially here, where the direct relationship to the client is an immanent factor and, thereby, a basic prerequisite for the success of a Personal Trainer, achieving a high retention rate should be a key strategy. In addition, the costs of gaining new clients are comparably high. To convince a potential customer of the abstract and personal as well as in relation to gym memberships comparably cost-intensive service, selling Personal Training needs a comparably higher investment of time and in marketing.

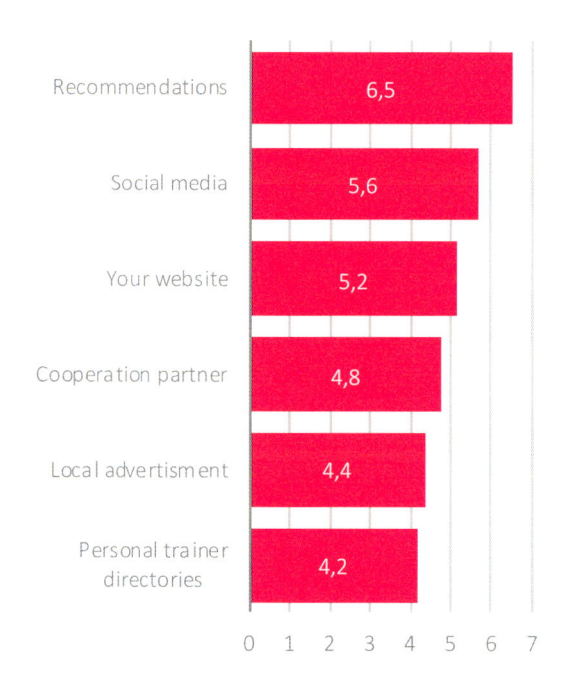

Channel	Score
Recommendations	6,5
Social media	5,6
Your website	5,2
Cooperation partner	4,8
Local advertisment	4,4
Personal trainer directories	4,2

Figure 2.51: Marketing channels of Personal Trainers.

Personal Training in Europe

By far the most relevant marketing channel for Personal Trainers is direct recommendation. On a scale from 0 to 7 the participating Personal Trainers rated recommendation with a 6.5 as the most important way to gain new clients. In second place are the social media activities of Personal Trainers. This comparably new channel is rated more relevant than the other marketing efforts. These two most relevant marketing channels are followed by the website of the trainer, cooperation with partners, local advertisement, and Personal Trainer directories, which are the lowest in the ranking.

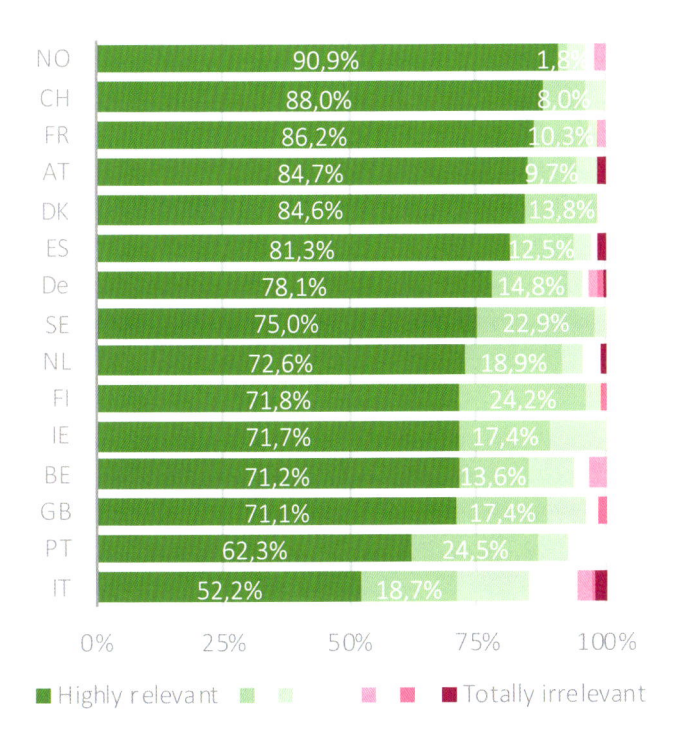

Country	Highly relevant	Totally irrelevant
NO	90,9%	1,8%
CH	88,0%	8,0%
FR	86,2%	10,3%
AT	84,7%	9,7%
DK	84,6%	13,8%
ES	81,3%	12,5%
De	78,1%	14,8%
SE	75,0%	22,9%
NL	72,6%	18,9%
FI	71,8%	24,2%
IE	71,7%	17,4%
BE	71,2%	13,6%
GB	71,1%	17,4%
PT	62,3%	24,5%
IT	52,2%	18,7%

Figure 2.52: National details on recommendations.

The strong rating of recommendations is also confirmed in the national context. The vast majority of Personal Trainers in the individual countries assess winning new clients through already existing clients or other contacts as the most important strategy. In Norway, more than 90% rate this as highly relevant. Only in the two Southern European states Portugal and Spain does the importance rating seem to be slightly lower with a perception of 62.3% and 52.2% respectively as highly relevant.

The difference between the importance of recommendations to the second ranked social media also becomes evident when looking at the national situation. Here, a maximum of 53.4% rate social media as highly relevant, which is almost 40 percentage points lower than the assessment of the top marketing channel recommendations. Also, in social media the ratings vary amongst the individual countries. While in France, Finland, and Denmark more than half of the trainers assess social media as highly relevant, in Germany, Portugal, and especially Belgium only around 30% do so.

FR	53,4%	20,7%
FI	52,0%	23,6%
DK	50,8%	21,5%
AT	49,3%	17,8%
NO	49,1%	12,7%
CH	48,9%	23,4%
IT	41,4%	30,8%
IE	39,1%	28,3%
NL	37,5%	24,0%
ES	36,3%	32,5%
SE	36,2%	23,4%
GB	35,1%	11,5%
DE	30,9%	21,0%
PT	30,4%	19,6%
BE	27,9%	36,8%

■ Highly relevant ■ ■ ■ ■ ■ Totally irreleva[nt]

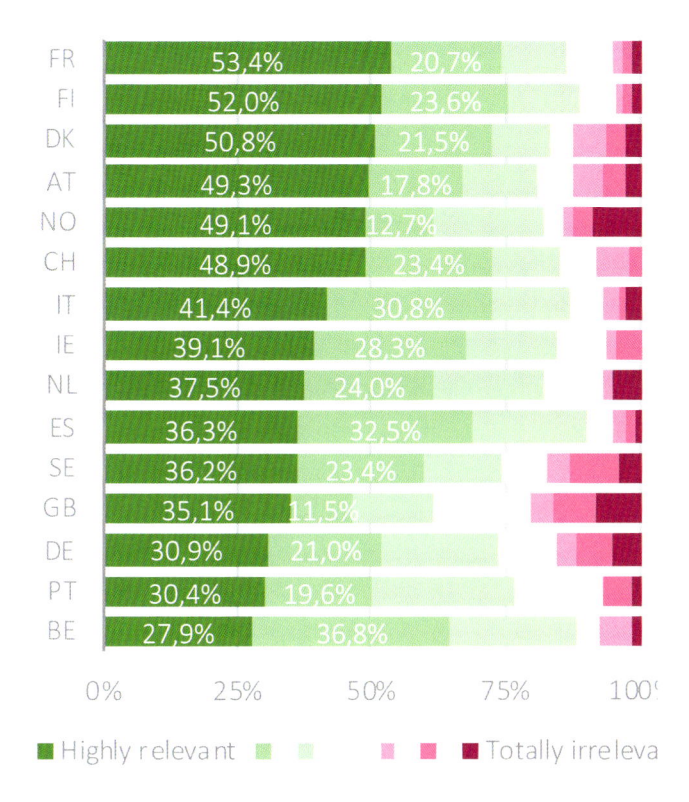

Figure 2.53: National details on social media.

2.6 Threats and Opportunities

Besides the total number of market participants, either in absolute numbers or in relation to, for instance, the population, the assessment of the respective relevant competitive landscape helps to evaluate a specific market. With respect to Personal Training, the survey-participants assess the Portuguese market as the one with the strongest competition from other trainers. Even though only a rather small number of respondents assess the competition as very strong more than 70% state it to be strong in Portugal. The United Kingdom and Denmark rank second and third with regard to their competitiveness in the Personal Training market. The markets with the least competitive landscape are Sweden, Italy, and Belgium. In the last, only 35.2% of the participating Personal Trainers assess competition to be strong and only 1.5% very strong.

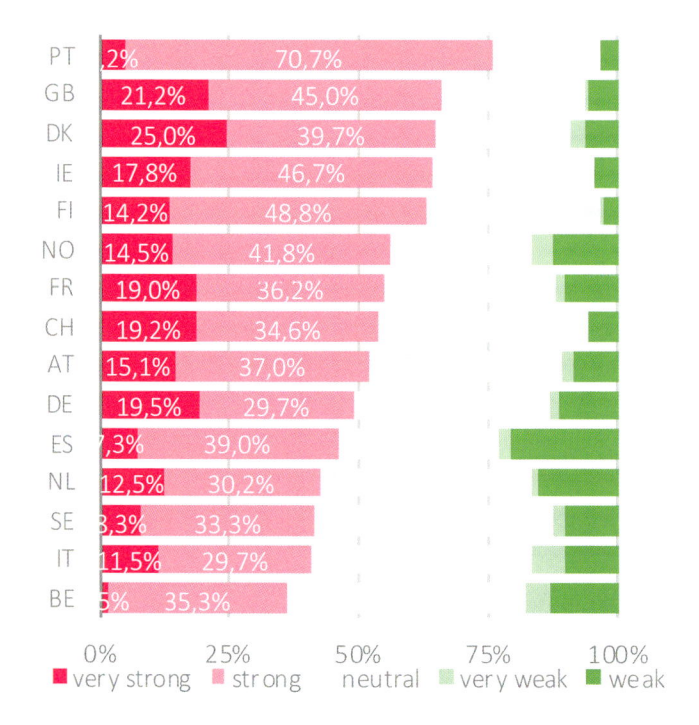

Country	very strong	strong
PT	2%	70,7%
GB	21,2%	45,0%
DK	25,0%	39,7%
IE	17,8%	46,7%
FI	14,2%	48,8%
NO	14,5%	41,8%
FR	19,0%	36,2%
CH	19,2%	34,6%
AT	15,1%	37,0%
DE	19,5%	29,7%
ES	7,3%	39,0%
NL	12,5%	30,2%
SE	3,3%	33,3%
IT	11,5%	29,7%
BE	5%	35,3%

Figure 2.54: Assessment of the competitive landscape.

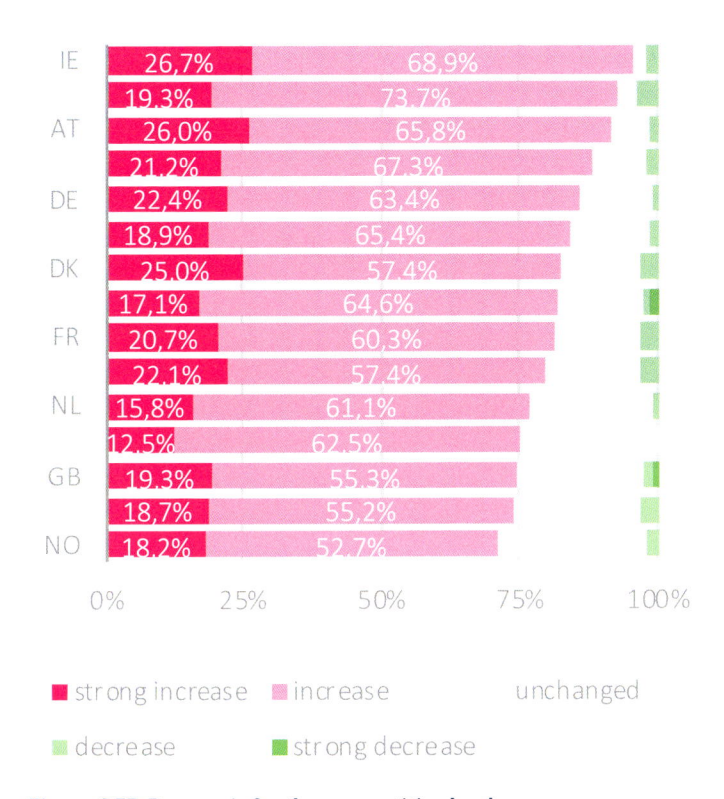

Figure 2.55: Prognosis for the competitive landscape.

A different and even clearer picture appears when the participants give their prognoses for the future development of competition in Personal Training. In every country at least 71% of the trainers expect an increase in competition. While in Norway, Italy, and the United Kingdom 70% to 75% expect an increase, these numbers are 92% and more in Austria, Portugal and Ireland.

Threat	Rating
Competition with other personal trainers	3,5
Changes in taxation	3,2
Online fitness offerings	3,2
Legal changes (e.g. labor law)	3,0
Health technology (e.g. wearables, apps for self-motivation)	2,9
Budget operators	2,9
Outdoor offerings	2,9
Boutique clubs	2,7
Competition with physio therapists	2,7

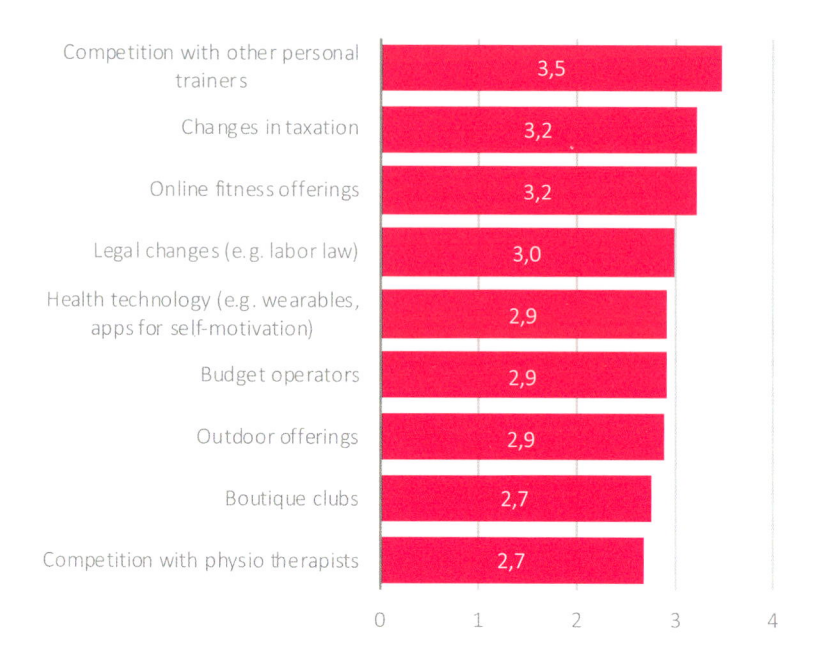

Figure 2.56: Individual threats for Personal Training.

Survey participants rate the growing competition with other Personal Trainers as the biggest threat to their own business. On a scale from 0 to 5, the factor competition amongst Personal Trainers is assessed with 3.5. Second and third rank changes in taxation and online fitness offerings, were both rated with 3.2.

Only minor differences are seen between the potential threats of legal changes, health technology, budget operators, or outdoor offerings. Boutique clubs as well as physio therapists are seen as the weakest threats in comparison to the others.

Compared to the individual threats, participating Personal Trainers rate the relevance of the respective opportunities significantly higher. All assessed opportunities, except the possible target group of younger people, at least at the same level as the strongest threat.

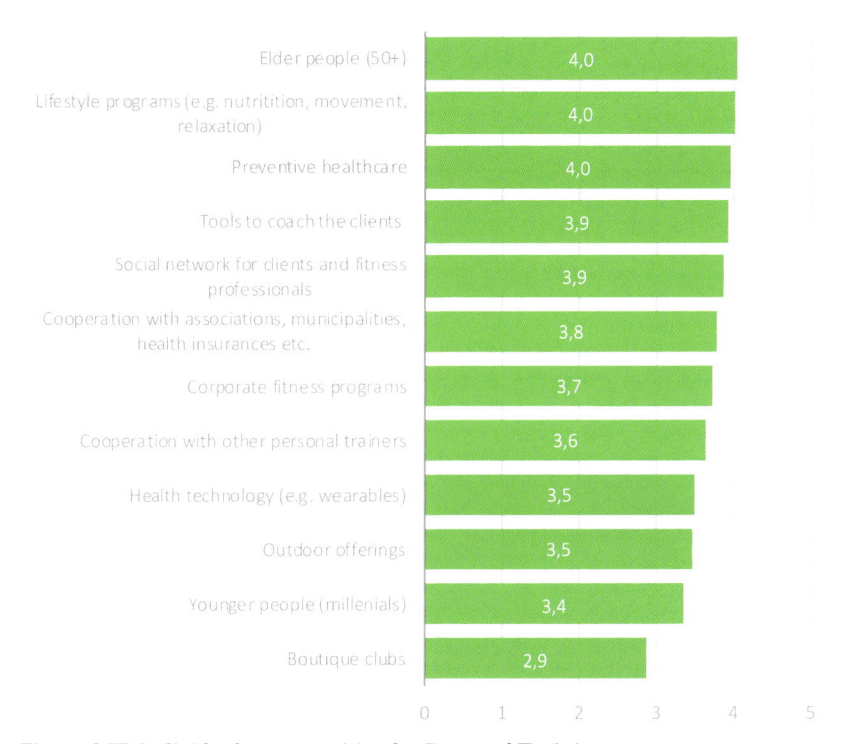

Opportunity	Rating
Elder people (50+)	4,0
Lifestyle programs (e.g. nutritition, movement, relaxation)	4,0
Preventive healthcare	4,0
Tools to coach the clients	3,9
Social network for clients and fitness professionals	3,9
Cooperation with associations, municipalities, health insurances etc.	3,8
Corporate fitness programs	3,7
Cooperation with other personal trainers	3,6
Health technology (e.g. wearables)	3,5
Outdoor offerings	3,5
Younger people (millenials)	3,4
Boutique clubs	2,9

Figure 2.57: Individual opportunities for Personal Training.

Thereby, elder people, lifestyle programs, and preventive healthcare are seen as the opportunities with the highest relevance of 4.0. The opportunities resulting from outdoor offerings and health technology are rated at least with 3.5.

2.7 Summary

This EuropeActive study on the state of Personal Training in 15 European countries was executed for two major reasons: First, we felt that Personal Training is an exciting and growing niche of the overall fitness market with a high level of popularity and penetration in some markets like the United States or the United Kingdom. Second, despite this growing interest the existing research and information on Personal Training are scarce.

To try and answer the basic question of how many Personal Trainers offer their services in Europe and the different national markets is not an easy task. Neither the term "Personal Training" is strictly defined nor "Personal Trainer" is a protected title. Moreover, Personal Training is not consistently organised across markets. To get at least an initial picture of the market size of Personal Training in different countries, we have applied the numbers of the business- and employment-oriented social networking service LinkedIn. Even though the individual figures have to be interpreted carefully, they do allow a basic comparison between the different countries and an initial assessment of the European Personal Training market.

We find the highest market penetration in Ireland and in the United Kingdom. The Personal Training markets in the German speaking countries, that is in Germany, Austria, and Switzerland, are less developed, but according to our approach have significantly more Personal Trainers in relation to their inhabitants than Spain and France which came last.

In order to explore the characteristics of the Personal Trainers their offerings and prices, their clients and marketing activities, as well as their assessment of threats and opportunities we set up an online survey as the core part of our research. A total of 4,370 fitness professionals participated in the online survey. 3,944 of them are located in the focused 15 European markets, and 2,819 of these are Personal Trainers.

In thirteen countries the portion of male trainers is higher than the share of female Personal Trainers. Finland and Norway are the only exceptions to this rule in our sample. It will be interesting to see whether the share of female Personal Trainers in the individual fitness markets will increase in the future.

Personal Trainers are a rather young group of professionals. Two major factors might influence this distribution. On the one hand, Personal Training itself is a rather "young" offering that is still developing. On the other hand, Personal Training is mostly related to doing sports and being active within the role of a trainer. The time participants have spent in their role as Personal Trainers as well as generally in the health and fitness industry, accordingly, are rather small.

Major cities seem to record a strong share of the overall number of Personal Trainers. The essential reason for this concentration of Personal Trainers is surely the higher absolute presence of the relevant target group in the larger cities. Therefore, it seems unlikely that this relationship will differ significantly between the individual markets or that it will change significantly as the Personal Training market develops.

The most important motivation to start working as a Personal Trainer is the general interest in sport and fitness, followed by helping people, and turning hobby into a career. Most of our respondents are generally satisfied with their decision and their work as a Personal Trainer. The "happiest" trainers are based in the Netherlands, Germany, and Austria. The most important reason for this generally high satisfaction level is seen in the possibility to help people, followed by fun of working in the field of sports, and the potential for development.

Based on our survey, fulltime and parttime employment of Personal Trainers seem to be relatively evenly distributed in the industry. The huge majority of them works self-employed. On average, the participating Personal Trainers have a maximum availability of 21.4 hours for Personal Training sessions per week. The portion of the effective Personal Training session at the total work to be done varies between the individual countries from almost 30% to more than 50%.

Based on the individual market situations, obviously different levels of revenue are realized by Personal Trainers in the individual countries. Reasons for these differences can be, amongst others, the achievable prices in a country or the level of competition on the one hand. On the other hand, also the different shares of fulltime and parttime Personal Trainers have their impact. The by far highest net revenues are realized in Switzerland, followed by Germany and Norway. The lowest average revenue is achieved in Portugal, Austria and Finland. While male Personal Trainers achieve an average of 2,152 EUR per month in Europe, the average of female Personal Trainers is only 1,371 EUR or 781 EUR less.

It is generally accepted that a good education is the essential prerequisite for a successful Personal Trainer. Especially in a service-based offering like Personal Training, an adequate education is a strong selling proposition and also a requirement for customer retention. The official educational requirements, however, differ strongly from country to country. While a Personal Trainer does not need any formal education at all to call himself a "Personal Trainer" in some countries, in others specific minimum requirements have to be fulfilled.

At the same time, the educational offerings of the individual national training providers also vary greatly. When looking at the highest level of education achieved by the participating Personal Trainers, it becomes evident that comprehensive fitness-related vocational programmes are the most commonly provided educational level in most of the countries. Even though the analysis unveils a highly heterogeneous and opaque landscape of educational offerings in the different countries, it also shows that only a very limited number of Personal Trainers has no certified fitness-related qualification.

More than half of the participating Personal Trainers state to invest between 26 and 100 hours per year into on-going education.

When asked what the important skills for Personal Trainers are, 85.7% of the participants answered personality skills followed by the willingness to learn and customer service skills. The hard facts, namely specific technical skills are ranked only sixth.

Against the background of the somewhat complex international educational system in the fitness industry, a majority of Personal Trainers assesses international standards as useful. One driving force for the development of international standards, not only for Personal Trainers but fitness professionals in general, is the European Register of Exercise Professionals as part of the European health and fitness association, EuropeActive. Our study reveals some growth potential for EREPS's awareness together with the development of international standards in selected European countries.

As interesting as characterising the Personal Trainers is the examination of their offering. Three different services stand out in the Personal Training portfolio: 89.1% of the participating trainers offer muscle development training and 78.7% cardio training, which can obviously be seen as the core services of a Personal Trainer. As expected, the "traditional" 1-on-1 training has the greatest importance in the work of Personal Trainers. At the same time, it seems to be the prevailing case that the client has to get to the trainer more often than the other way around, when it comes to the location where the Personal Training services are offered.

Based on our research, the average price for a 1-on-1 session is 53 EUR. The price female Personal Trainers charge is higher than the price of their male colleagues. While women on average charge 60 EUR, it is 50 EUR when the trainers are men. To some extent it could be explained by the large number of male Personal Trainers in countries with comparably lower price levels such as Italy and Spain. The lowest average price is seen in the three South-European countries Italy, Spain, and Portugal together with Ireland. In all four countries the average price is 35 EUR. By far the highest average price for a 1-on-1 session is realised in Switzerland with 119 EUR.

Beyond the description of the actual prices of Personal Training in the individual markets, the relation of the prices to specific parameters is worth examining. The highest fitness-related qualification achieved by a Personal Trainer seems to have a positive impact on the price to be charged by Personal Trainers. While Personal Trainers with a basic qualification charge 53.30 EUR the price increases with higher levels of education. Also, the respective experience as well as the external factor of the size of the city a Personal Trainer is working in has an impact on the price of Personal Training sessions.

The vast majority of Personal Trainer sees an increasing usage and importance of technology in their field. Today, the most used piece of technology amongst Personal Trainers is the smartphone, followed by computers and laptops, timers, tablets, and wearables.

One of the obviously most interesting aspects in the field of Personal Training is the clients. However, as we have conducted a survey only amongst the trainers within our research, we could only rely on this indirect assessment of the clients, here. Based on our survey, the majority of Personal Training clients are women. On international average, almost two-thirds of all clients are female. When looking at the distribution of clients into different age groups, it becomes evident that more than half of the clients are in the group of the 30- to-49-year-old. The age groups 30 to 39 and 40 to 49 are relatively equally distributed. The often-proclaimed trend towards the older customer groups and their market power does not seem to have affected the Personal Training market significantly so far.

By far the most important goal in Personal Training is weight loss. Two-thirds of the trainers see losing weight as the most important aim of their clients. It is followed by get fit, get toned/build muscle and be healthy. Thereby, the most frequent reason to choose a Personal Trainer is a lack of knowledge about how to exercise correctly. The inability to commit to a plan or missing self-discipline, both of which have their roots in the motivation of the client, also bring clients to Personal Trainers as well as a lack of visible results in the past, which is seen as another important reason by the Personal Trainers.

Another view on Personal Training clients is the operational perspective of the trainers. With respect to the total number of clients the clear majority of Personal Trainers have a maximum of 25 clients. The most prevalent number of training sessions is one to three times a week. It is interesting that not more than 5.2% of the clients book a session with a Personal Trainer only once. Obviously, Personal Trainers are mostly able to convince their customers to continue their joint work after an initial trial session.

In this regard, the direct relationship to the client is a basic prerequisite for the success of a Personal Trainer, achieving a high retention rate should be a key strategy. Thus, by far the most relevant marketing channel for Personal Trainers is direct recommendation. In second place are the social media activities of Personal Trainers.

The more competitive the market, the more important are marketing activities. In all 15 countries, at least 71% of the trainers expect an increase in competition. Survey participants rate the growing competition with other Personal Trainers as the biggest threat to their own business. At the same time, Personal Trainers rate the relevance of various opportunities significantly higher: elder people, lifestyle programs, and preventive healthcare are seen as the top opportunities for the Personal Training market in future.

In the context of limited information and lacking research, we consider our study to be exploratory. We believe it is a valuable starting point and call for additional research on the fundamental question of market sizes as well as on all the other factors we examined in our work.

As already indicated, our approach to approximate market sizes and penetrations has it shortcomings. Integrating the LinkedIn basis for the total number of Personal Trainers might not always deliver accurate numbers. However, only little to no reliable data was available before we started our work. Using these numbers at least delivers a comparable set of data and an initial indication for the different markets. When replicating our approach in future we should be able to benefit from the growing market penetration of LinkedIn in Europe. Apart from such a replication we will continue and enhance our efforts to motivate relevant major market players such as associations, education providers, or operators to join forces for a direct measurement of market figures.

Our main analysis established a solid foundation for the understanding of the characteristics of the Personal Trainers and for the details of their offerings and prices. We gained first insights into Personal Trainers' clients and marketing activities and touched upon threats and opportunities the Personal Trainers observe and expect in their market. A further edition of our study is needed to confirm the results of our initial analysis of the Personal Training segment as well as to potentially show changes and development over time in the respective parameters.

Moreover, it will be interesting to check whether the opportunities that Personal Trainers see actually will materialise and, thus, change the market conditions. Furthermore, we cannot wait to see whether the trends our current data together with general observations in the market suggest do become reality. Special attention shall be given to the expected growing importance of older targets groups, the predicted increase in the portion of female Personal Trainers, or the establishment of standards in the educational system for fitness professionals many market players long for.

In our current work, the breaking down of the individual parameters into every detail on a national basis is limited by the number of achieved participants in the respective countries. Therefore, additional research especially on a national level for the respective countries will be necessary to further develop this interesting field of research. In future, we hope to achieve a stronger participation in all countries through an even stronger engagement of multiplying partners. From our side, we will be happy to continue our work on Personal Training and are looking forward to any future cooperation in this regard.

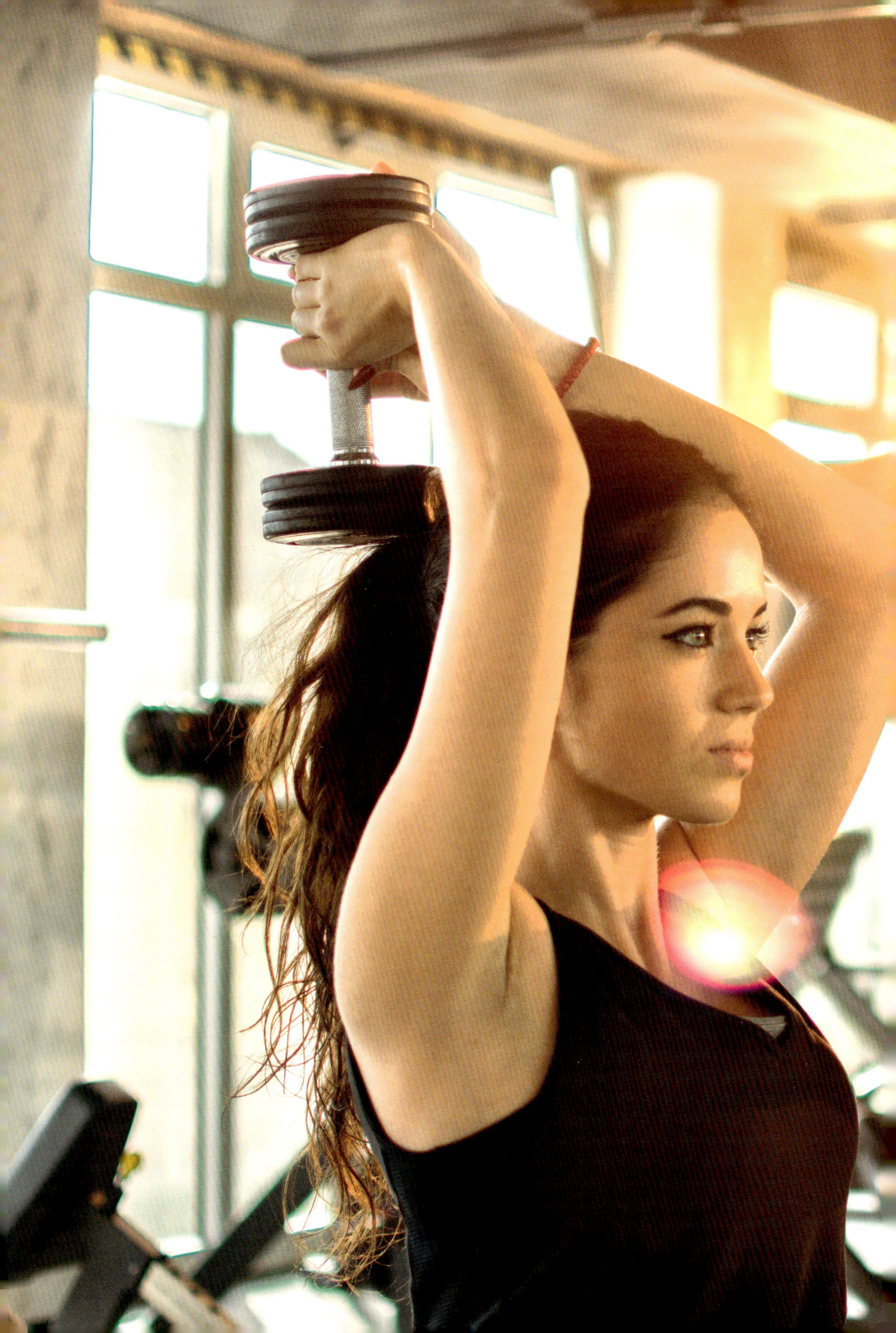

3 National Data Compilation

Austria

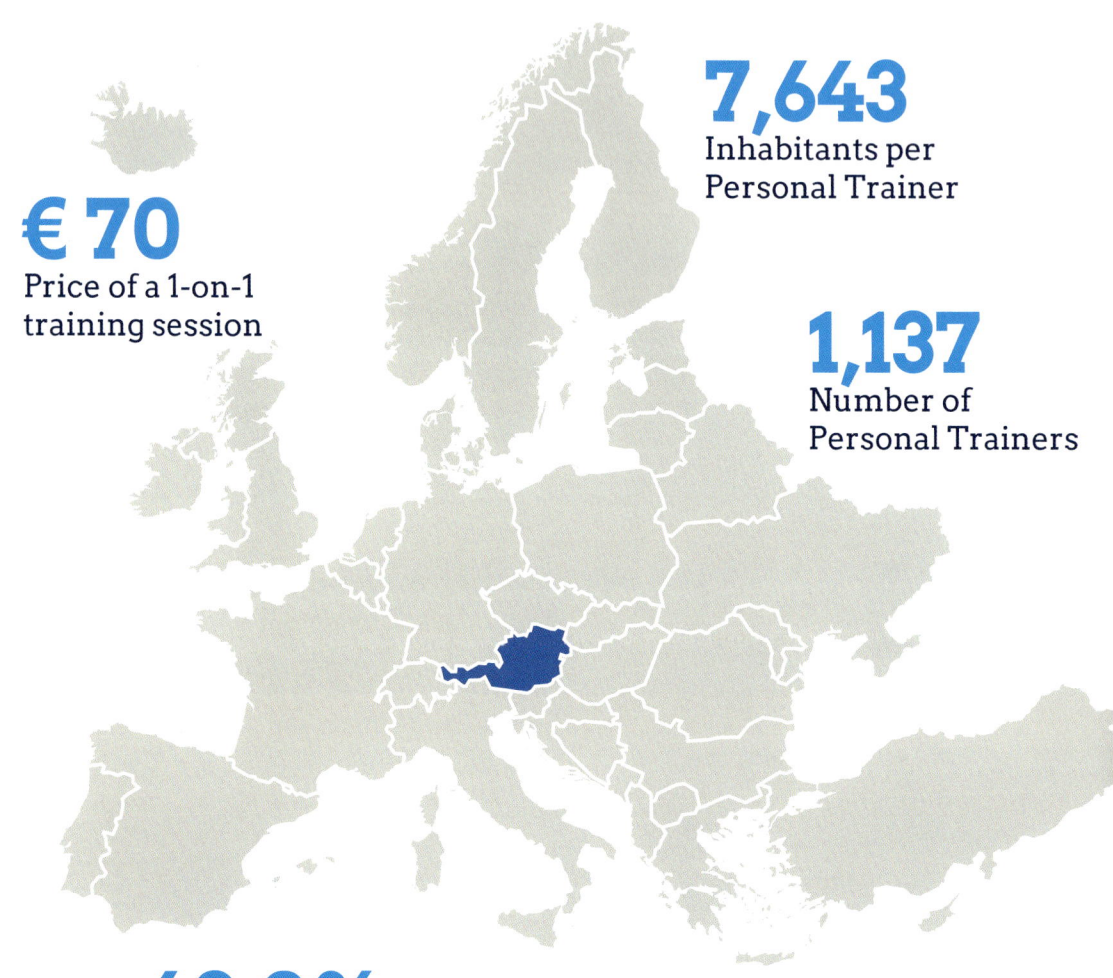

7,643
Inhabitants per Personal Trainer

€ 70
Price of a 1-on-1 training session

1,137
Number of Personal Trainers

42.0%
Portion of fulltime Personal Trainers

47.6%
Portion female Personal Trainers

Personal Training in Europe

General Market Information	
Total general population	8.690.076
Number of Personal Trainers	1.137
Inhabitants per Personal Trainer	7.643
15 countries' average	5.772
Number of participating Personal Trainers	147
Participation rate	12,9%
15 countries' average	4,0%
Market share of cities > 250,000 inhabitants	60,5%
15 countries' average	42,7%
Portion of competition assessment as "strong" or "very strong"	52,1%
15 countries' average	52,7%
Portion of competition prognosis as "increase" or "strong increase"	91,8%
15 countries' average	81,0%

Offering	
Portion of 1-on-1 training	59,7%
Portion of 1-on-2 training	12,1%
Portion of small group training	28,2%
15 countries' average for 1-on-1 training	72,4%
Price of a 1-on-1 training session (in EUR p.p.)	70
Price of a 1-on-2 training session (in EUR p.p.)	50
Price of a small group training session (in EUR p.p.)	15
15 countries' average for the price of a 1-on-1 training session (in EUR p.p.)	53

Personal Trainer	
Portion female Personal Trainers	47,6%
15 countries' average	36,1%
In absolute numbers	541
Average age of Personal Trainers (in years)	34
15 countries' average (in years)	34
Portion of fulltime Personal Trainers	42,0%
15 countries' average	46,3%
In absolute numbers	477
Portion of self-employed Personal Trainers	80,2%
15 countries' average	73,1%
In absolute numbers	911
Average time spent in industry (in years)	7
15 countries' average (in years)	9
Average time working as Personal Trainer (in years)	5
15 countries' average (in years)	6
Portion of Personal Trainers with a bachelor's degree or higher	23,9%
15 countries' average	32,2%
Portion of "very satisfied" Personal Trainers	47,8%
15 countries' average	37,6%
Average monthly net revenue (in EUR)	1.203
15 countries' average (in EUR)	1.894

Belgium

€ 50
Price of a 1-on-1 training session

8,499
Inhabitants per Personal Trainer

1,331
Number of Personal Trainers

48.9%
Portion of fulltime Personal Trainers

24.1%
Portion female Personal Trainers

Personal Training in Europe

General Market Information	
Total general population	11.311.117
Number of Personal Trainers	1.331
Inhabitants per Personal Trainer	8.499
15 countries' average	5.772
Number of participating Personal Trainers	137
Participation rate	10,3%
15 countries' average	4,0%
Market share of cities > 250,000 inhabitants	29,9%
15 countries' average	42,7%
Portion of competition assessment as "strong" or "very strong"	36,8%
15 countries' average	52,7%
Portion of competition prognosis as "increase" or "strong increase"	79,4%
15 countries' average	81,0%

Offering	
Portion of 1-on-1 training	74,1%
Portion of 1-on-2 training	11,4%
Portion of small group training	14,5%
15 countries' average for 1-on-1 training	72,4%
Price of a 1-on-1 training session (in EUR p.p.)	50
Price of a 1-on-2 training session (in EUR p.p.)	30
Price of a small group training session (in EUR p.p.)	15
15 countries' average for the price of a 1-on-1 training session (in EUR p.p.)	53

Personal Trainer	
Portion female Personal Trainers	24,1%
15 countries' average	36,1%
In absolute numbers	321
Average age of Personal Trainers (in years)	35
15 countries' average (in years)	34
Portion of fulltime Personal Trainers	48,9%
15 countries' average	46,3%
In absolute numbers	650
Portion of self-employed Personal Trainers	92,5%
15 countries' average	73,1%
In absolute numbers	1.232
Average time spent in industry (in years)	8
15 countries' average (in years)	9
Average time working as Personal Trainer (in years)	5
15 countries' average (in years)	6
Portion of Personal Trainers with a bachelor's degree or higher	35,7%
15 countries' average	32,2%
Portion of "very satisfied" Personal Trainers	43,9%
15 countries' average	37,6%
Average monthly net revenue (in EUR)	2.106
15 countries' average (in EUR)	1.894

Denmark

€ 77
Price of a 1-on-1 training session

14,637
Inhabitants per Personal Trainer

390
Number of Personal Trainers

32.1%
Portion of fulltime Personal Trainers

45.3%
Portion female Personal Trainers

Personal Training in Europe

General Market Information	
Total general population	5.707.251
Number of Personal Trainers	390
Inhabitants per Personal Trainer	14.637
15 countries' average	5.772
Number of participating Personal Trainers	161
Participation rate	41,3%
15 countries' average	4,0%
Market share of cities > 250,000 inhabitants	45,3%
15 countries' average	42,7%
Portion of competition assessment as "strong" or "very strong"	64,7%
15 countries' average	52,7%
Portion of competition prognosis as "increase" or "strong increase"	82,4%
15 countries' average	81,0%

Offering	
Portion of 1-on-1 training	75,9%
Portion of 1-on-2 training	9,0%
Portion of small group training	15,1%
15 countries' average for 1-on-1 training	72,4%
Price of a 1-on-1 training session (in EUR p.p.)	77
Price of a 1-on-2 training session (in EUR p.p.)	60
Price of a small group training session (in EUR p.p.)	40
15 countries' average for the price of a 1-on-1 training session (in EUR p.p.)	53

Personal Trainer	
Portion female Personal Trainers	45,3%
15 countries' average	36,1%
In absolute numbers	177
Average age of Personal Trainers (in years)	34
15 countries' average (in years)	34
Portion of fulltime Personal Trainers	32,1%
15 countries' average	46,3%
In absolute numbers	125
Portion of self-employed Personal Trainers	55,8%
15 countries' average	73,1%
In absolute numbers	217
Average time spent in industry (in years)	7
15 countries' average (in years)	9
Average time working as Personal Trainer (in years)	4
15 countries' average (in years)	6
Portion of Personal Trainers with a bachelor's degree or higher	24,6%
15 countries' average	32,2%
Portion of "very satisfied" Personal Trainers	38,8%
15 countries' average	37,6%
Average monthly net revenue (in EUR)	1.951
15 countries' average (in EUR)	1.894

Finland

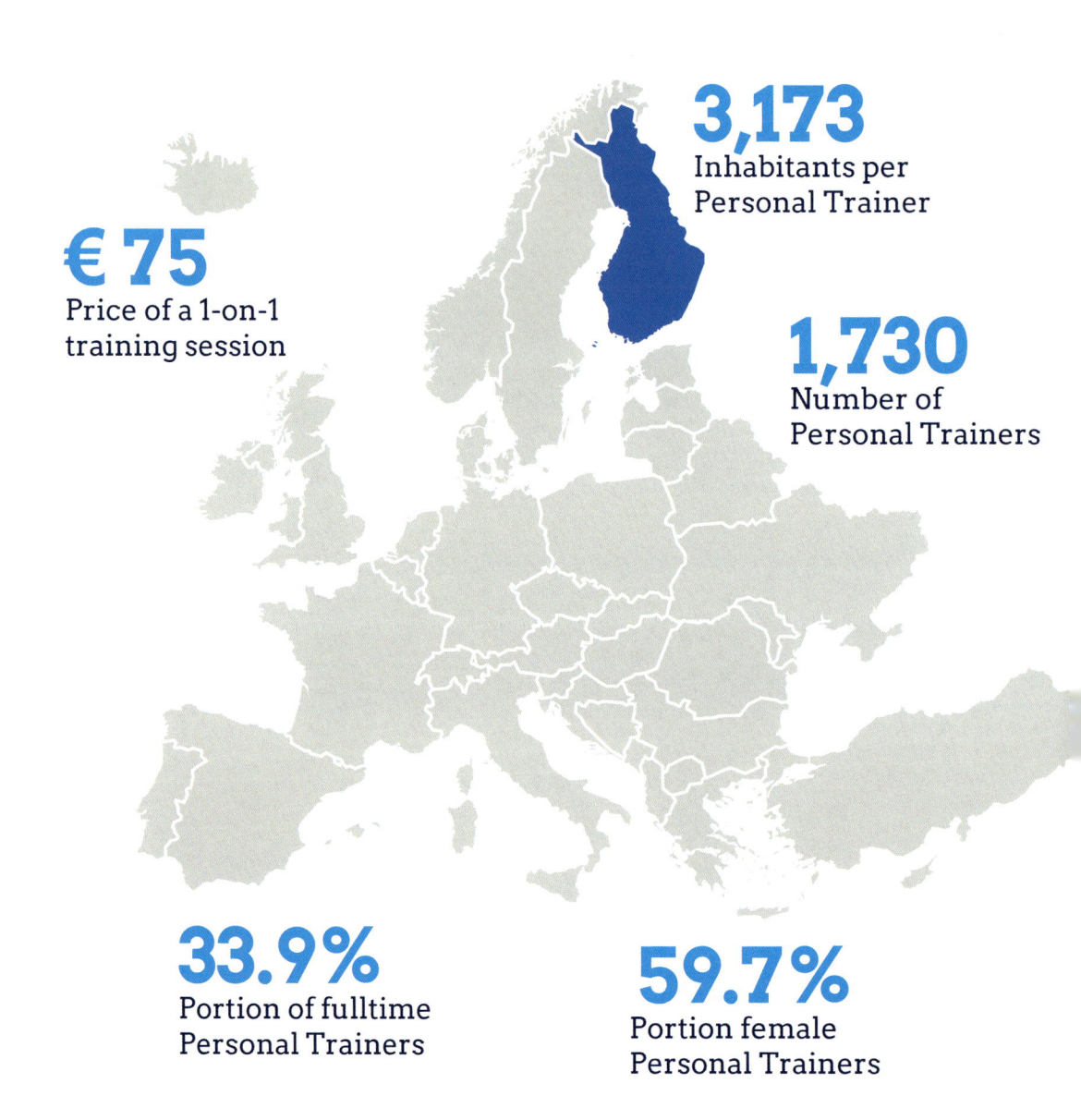

3,173
Inhabitants per Personal Trainer

€ 75
Price of a 1-on-1 training session

1,730
Number of Personal Trainers

33.9%
Portion of fulltime Personal Trainers

59.7%
Portion female Personal Trainers

Personal Training in Europe

General Market Information	
Total general population	5.487.308
Number of Personal Trainers	1.730
Inhabitants per Personal Trainer	3.173
15 countries' average	5.772
Number of participating Personal Trainers	226
Participation rate	13,1%
15 countries' average	4,0%
Market share of cities > 250,000 inhabitants	36,4%
15 countries' average	42,7%
Portion of competition assessment as "strong" or "very strong"	63,0%
15 countries' average	52,7%
Portion of competition prognosis as "increase" or "strong increase"	84,3%
15 countries' average	81,0%

Offering	
Portion of 1-on-1 training	73,6%
Portion of 1-on-2 training	7,0%
Portion of small group training	19,4%
15 countries' average for 1-on-1 training	72,4%
Price of a 1-on-1 training session (in EUR p.p.)	75
Price of a 1-on-2 training session (in EUR p.p.)	60
Price of a small group training session (in EUR p.p.)	35
15 countries' average for the price of a 1-on-1 training session (in EUR p.p.)	53

Personal Trainer	
Portion female Personal Trainers	59,7%
15 countries' average	36,1%
In absolute numbers	1.033
Average age of Personal Trainers (in years)	38
15 countries' average (in years)	34
Portion of fulltime Personal Trainers	33,9%
15 countries' average	46,3%
In absolute numbers	587
Portion of self-employed Personal Trainers	74,9%
15 countries' average	73,1%
In absolute numbers	1.295
Average time spent in industry (in years)	8
15 countries' average (in years)	9
Average time working as Personal Trainer (in years)	5
15 countries' average (in years)	6
Portion of Personal Trainers with a bachelor's degree or higher	22,9%
15 countries' average	32,2%
Portion of "very satisfied" Personal Trainers	23,5%
15 countries' average	37,6%
Average monthly net revenue (in EUR)	1.139
15 countries' average (in EUR)	1.894

France

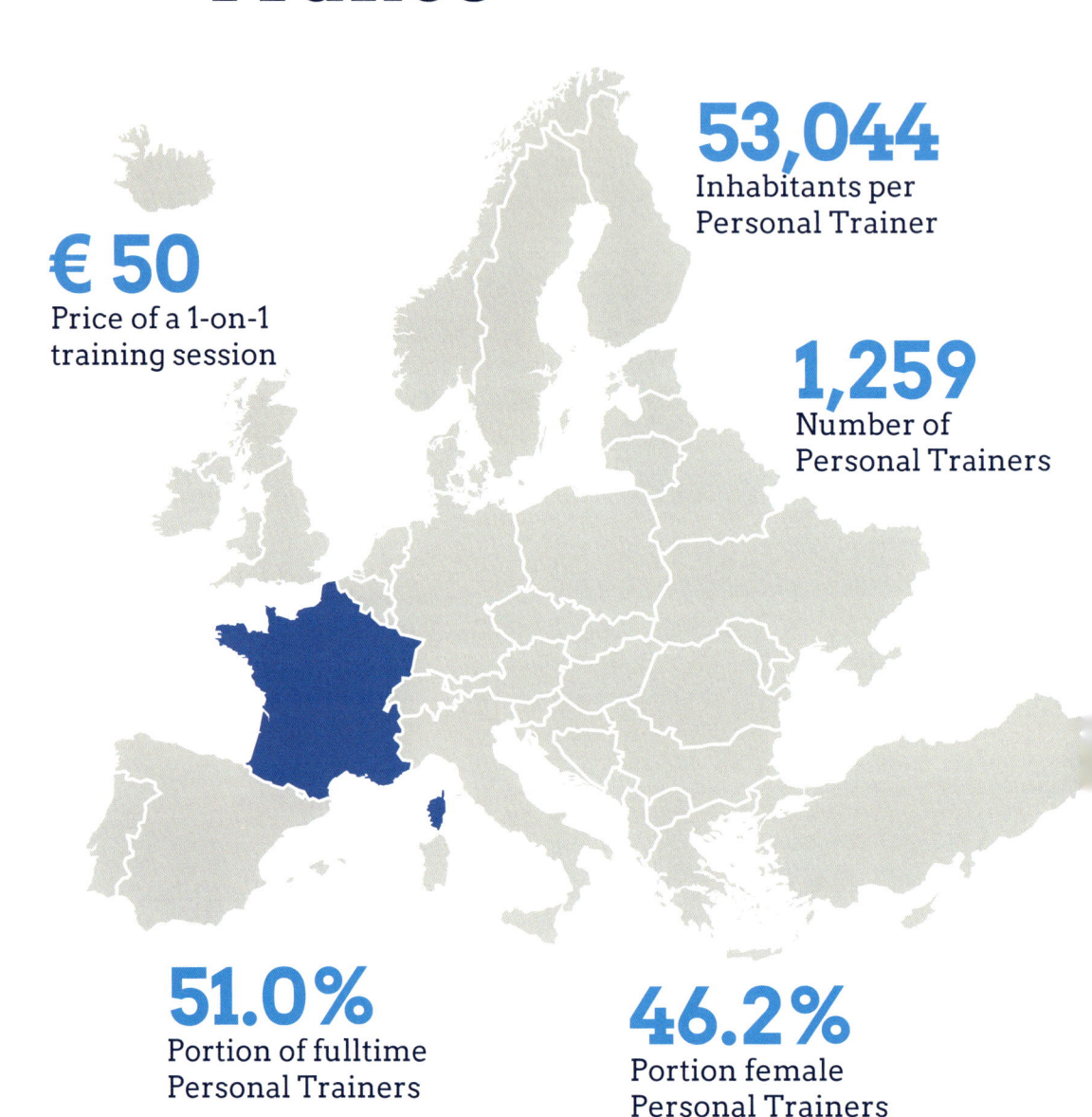

€ 50
Price of a 1-on-1 training session

53,044
Inhabitants per Personal Trainer

1,259
Number of Personal Trainers

51.0%
Portion of fulltime Personal Trainers

46.2%
Portion female Personal Trainers

Personal Training in Europe

General Market Information	
Total general population	66.759.950
Number of Personal Trainers	1.259
Inhabitants per Personal Trainer	53.044
15 countries' average	5.772
Number of participating Personal Trainers	104
Participation rate	8,3%
15 countries' average	4,0%
Market share of cities > 250,000 inhabitants	42,3%
15 countries' average	42,7%
Portion of competition assessment as "strong" or "very strong"	55,2%
15 countries' average	52,7%
Portion of competition prognosis as "increase" or "strong increase"	81,0%
15 countries' average	81,0%

Offering	
Portion of 1-on-1 training	66,0%
Portion of 1-on-2 training	11,5%
Portion of small group training	22,5%
15 countries' average for 1-on-1 training	72,4%
Price of a 1-on-1 training session (in EUR p.p.)	50
Price of a 1-on-2 training session (in EUR p.p.)	35
Price of a small group training session (in EUR p.p.)	20
15 countries' average for the price of a 1-on-1 training session (in EUR p.p.)	53

Personal Trainer	
Portion female Personal Trainers	46,2%
15 countries' average	36,1%
In absolute numbers	581
Average age of Personal Trainers (in years)	35
15 countries' average (in years)	34
Portion of fulltime Personal Trainers	51,0%
15 countries' average	46,3%
In absolute numbers	642
Portion of self-employed Personal Trainers	75,0%
15 countries' average	73,1%
In absolute numbers	944
Average time spent in industry (in years)	8
15 countries' average (in years)	9
Average time working as Personal Trainer (in years)	5
15 countries' average (in years)	6
Portion of Personal Trainers with a bachelor's degree or higher	27,9%
15 countries' average	32,2%
Portion of "very satisfied" Personal Trainers	43,5%
15 countries' average	37,6%
Average monthly net revenue (in EUR)	1.403
15 countries' average (in EUR)	1.894

Germany

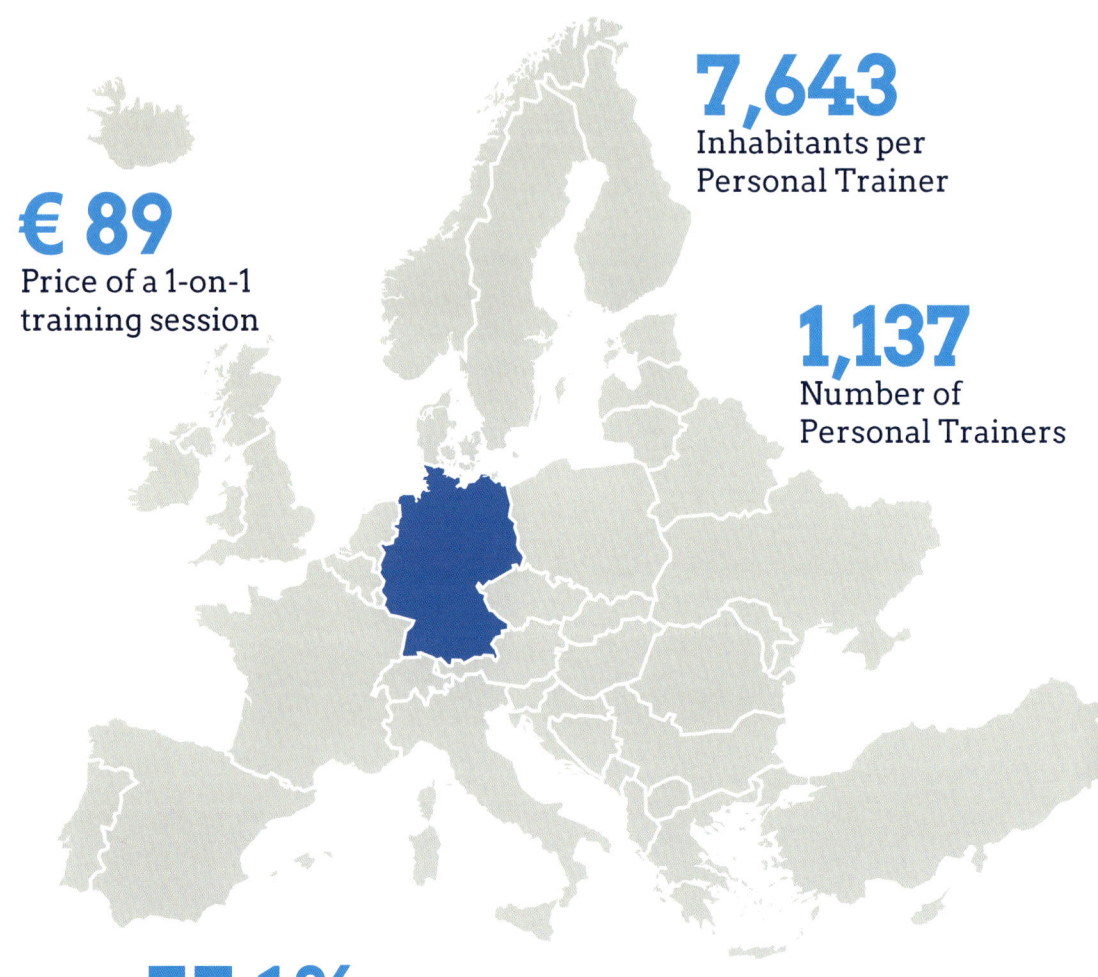

€ 89
Price of a 1-on-1 training session

7,643
Inhabitants per Personal Trainer

1,137
Number of Personal Trainers

55.1 %
Portion of fulltime Personal Trainers

36.4 %
Portion female Personal Trainers

Personal Training in Europe 149

General Market Information	
Total general population	82.175.684
Number of Personal Trainers	8.797
Inhabitants per Personal Trainer	9.341
15 countries' average	5.772
Number of participating Personal Trainers	302
Participation rate	3,4%
15 countries' average	4,0%
Market share of cities > 250,000 inhabitants	50,5%
15 countries' average	42,7%
Portion of competition assessment as "strong" or "very strong"	49,2%
15 countries' average	52,7%
Portion of competition prognosis as "increase" or "strong increase"	85,8%
15 countries' average	81,0%

Offering	
Portion of 1-on-1 training	75,1%
Portion of 1-on-2 training	9,1%
Portion of small group training	15,7%
15 countries' average for 1-on-1 training	72,4%
Price of a 1-on-1 training session (in EUR p.p.)	89
Price of a 1-on-2 training session (in EUR p.p.)	60
Price of a small group training session (in EUR p.p.)	30
15 countries' average for the price of a 1-on-1 training session (in EUR p.p.)	53

Personal Trainer	
Portion female Personal Trainers	36,4%
15 countries' average	36,1%
In absolute numbers	3.204
Average age of Personal Trainers (in years)	37
15 countries' average (in years)	34
Portion of fulltime Personal Trainers	55,1%
15 countries' average	46,3%
In absolute numbers	4.848
Portion of self-employed Personal Trainers	79,9%
15 countries' average	73,1%
In absolute numbers	7.032
Average time spent in industry (in years)	11
15 countries' average (in years)	9
Average time working as Personal Trainer (in years)	7
15 countries' average (in years)	6
Portion of Personal Trainers with a bachelor's degree or higher	26,2%
15 countries' average	32,2%
Portion of "very satisfied" Personal Trainers	45,1%
15 countries' average	37,6%
Average monthly net revenue (in EUR)	2.698
15 countries' average (in EUR)	1.894

Ireland

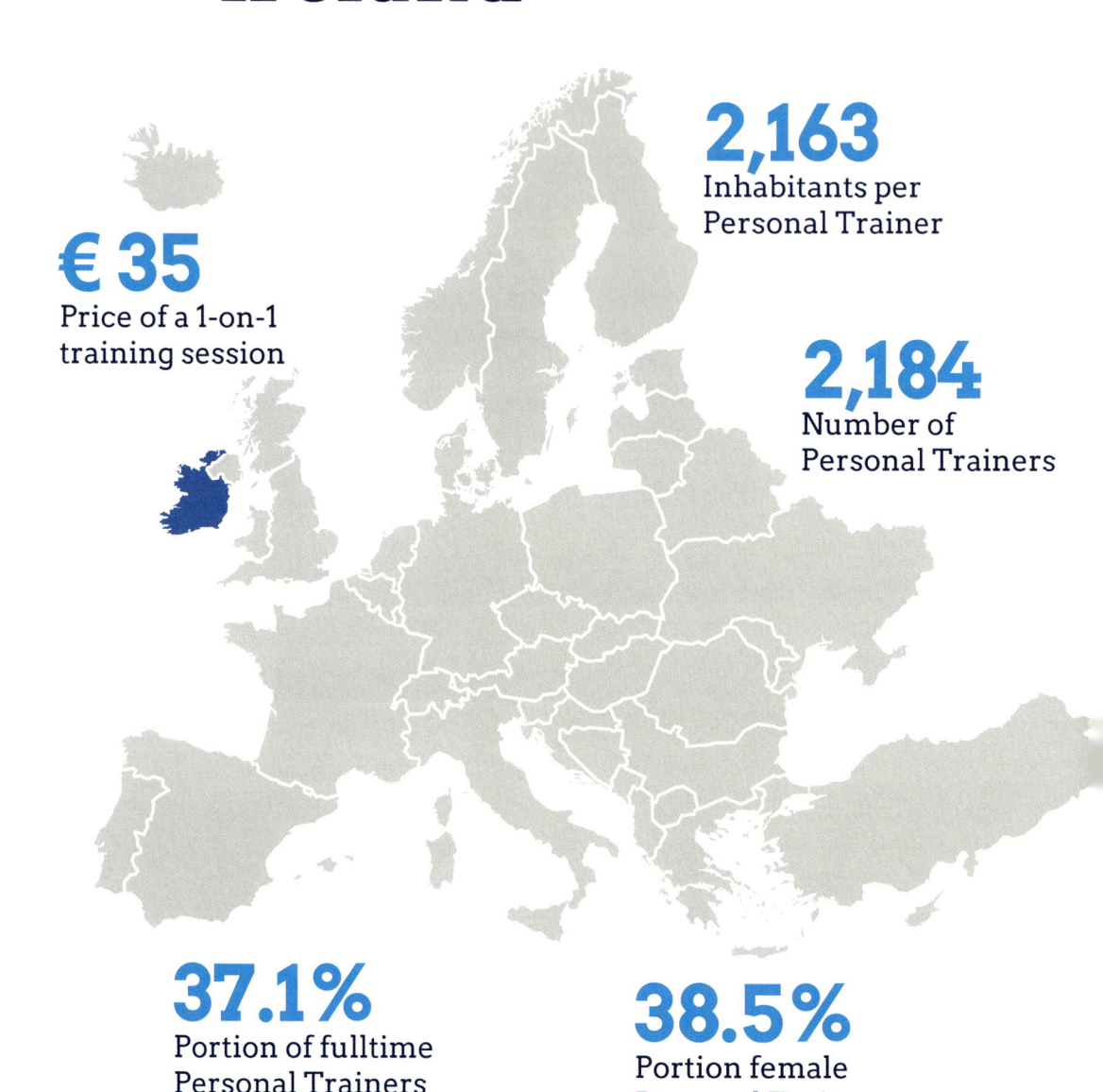

€ 35
Price of a 1-on-1 training session

2,163
Inhabitants per Personal Trainer

2,184
Number of Personal Trainers

37.1%
Portion of fulltime Personal Trainers

38.5%
Portion female Personal Trainers

Personal Training in Europe

General Market Information	
Total general population	4.724.720
Number of Personal Trainers	2.184
Inhabitants per Personal Trainer	2.163
15 countries' average	5.772
Number of participating Personal Trainers	109
Participation rate	5,0%
15 countries' average	4,0%
Market share of cities > 250,000 inhabitants	38,0%
15 countries' average	42,7%
Portion of competition assessment as "strong" or "very strong"	64,4%
15 countries' average	52,7%
Portion of competition prognosis as "increase" or "strong increase"	95,6%
15 countries' average	81,0%

Offering	
Portion of 1-on-1 training	63,1%
Portion of 1-on-2 training	13,6%
Portion of small group training	23,3%
15 countries' average for 1-on-1 training	72,4%
Price of a 1-on-1 training session (in EUR p.p.)	35
Price of a 1-on-2 training session (in EUR p.p.)	25
Price of a small group training session (in EUR p.p.)	16
15 countries' average for the price of a 1-on-1 training session (in EUR p.p.)	53

Personal Trainer	
Portion female Personal Trainers	38,5%
15 countries' average	36,1%
In absolute numbers	842
Average age of Personal Trainers (in years)	34
15 countries' average (in years)	34
Portion of fulltime Personal Trainers	37,1%
15 countries' average	46,3%
In absolute numbers	811
Portion of self-employed Personal Trainers	67,0%
15 countries' average	73,1%
In absolute numbers	1.463
Average time spent in industry (in years)	6
15 countries' average (in years)	9
Average time working as Personal Trainer (in years)	4
15 countries' average (in years)	6
Portion of Personal Trainers with a bachelor's degree or higher	18,8%
15 countries' average	32,2%
Portion of "very satisfied" Personal Trainers	44,7%
15 countries' average	37,6%
Average monthly net revenue (in EUR)	1.751
15 countries' average (in EUR)	1.894

Italy

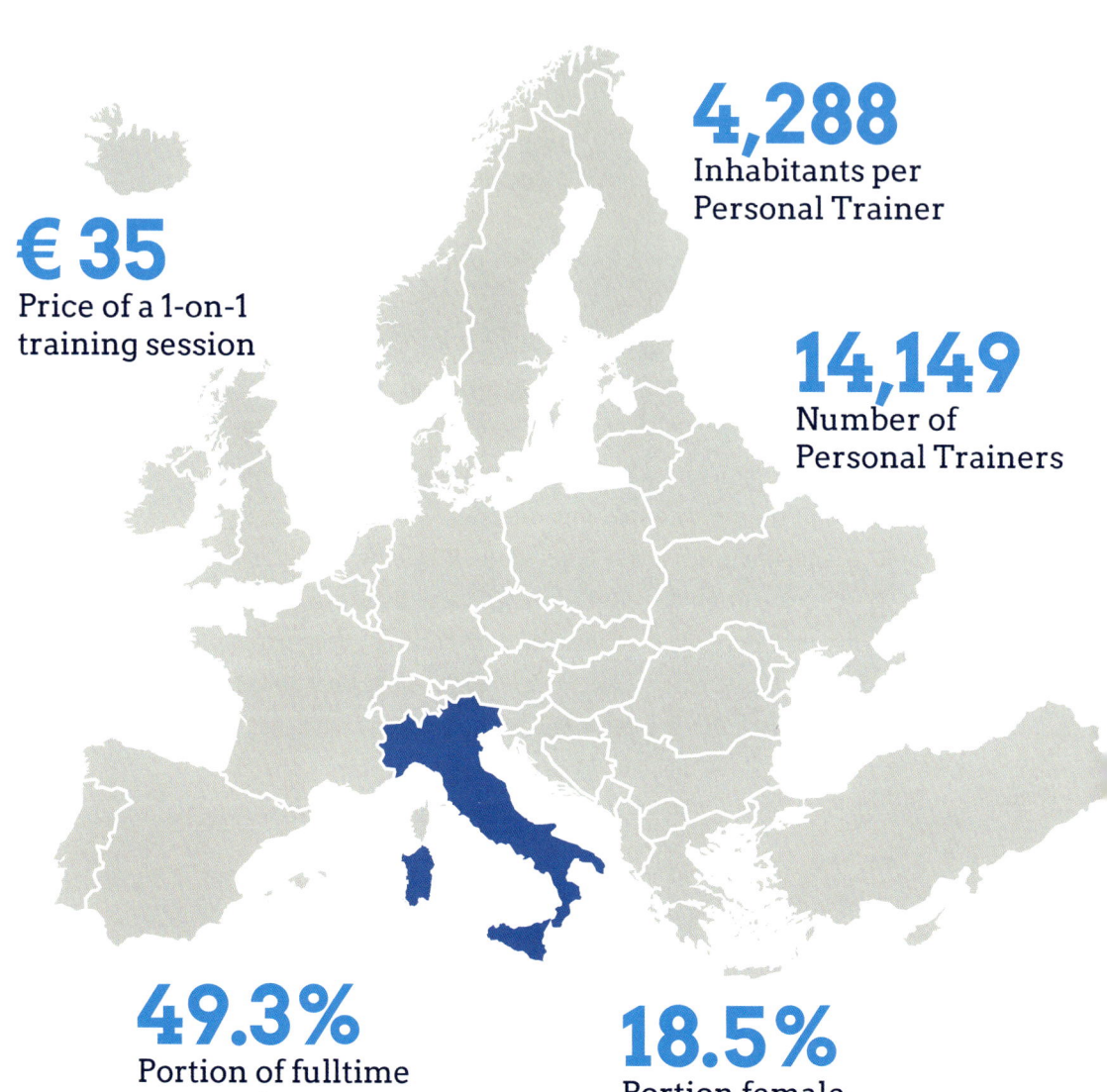

€ 35
Price of a 1-on-1 training session

4,288
Inhabitants per Personal Trainer

14,149
Number of Personal Trainers

49.3%
Portion of fulltime Personal Trainers

18.5%
Portion female Personal Trainers

Personal Training in Europe

General Market Information	
Total general population	60.665.551
Number of Personal Trainers	14.149
Inhabitants per Personal Trainer	4.288
15 countries' average	5.772
Number of participating Personal Trainers	500
Participation rate	3,5%
15 countries' average	4,0%
Market share of cities > 250,000 inhabitants	36,3%
15 countries' average	42,7%
Portion of competition assessment as "strong" or "very strong"	41,3%
15 countries' average	52,7%
Portion of competition prognosis as "increase" or "strong increase"	73,9%
15 countries' average	81,0%

Offering	
Portion of 1-on-1 training	70,4%
Portion of 1-on-2 training	10,9%
Portion of small group training	18,6%
15 countries' average for 1-on-1 training	72,4%
Price of a 1-on-1 training session (in EUR p.p.)	35
Price of a 1-on-2 training session (in EUR p.p.)	25
Price of a small group training session (in EUR p.p.)	15
15 countries' average for the price of a 1-on-1 training session (in EUR p.p.)	53

Personal Trainer	
Portion female Personal Trainers	18,5%
15 countries' average	36,1%
In absolute numbers	2.614
Average age of Personal Trainers (in years)	37
15 countries' average (in years)	34
Portion of fulltime Personal Trainers	49,3%
15 countries' average	46,3%
In absolute numbers	6.972
Portion of self-employed Personal Trainers	76,7%
15 countries' average	73,1%
In absolute numbers	10.859
Average time spent in industry (in years)	12
15 countries' average (in years)	9
Average time working as Personal Trainer (in years)	7
15 countries' average (in years)	6
Portion of Personal Trainers with a bachelor's degree or higher	42,7%
15 countries' average	32,2%
Portion of "very satisfied" Personal Trainers	33,6%
15 countries' average	37,6%
Average monthly net revenue (in EUR)	1.603
15 countries' average (in EUR)	1.894

The Netherlands

4,166
Inhabitants per Personal Trainer

€ 55
Price of a 1-on-1 training session

4,076
Number of Personal Trainers

47.8%
Portion of fulltime Personal Trainers

37.0%
Portion female Personal Trainers

Personal Training in Europe

General Market Information	
Total general population	16.979.120
Number of Personal Trainers	4.076
Inhabitants per Personal Trainer	4.166
15 countries' average	5.772
Number of participating Personal Trainers	184
Participation rate	4,5%
15 countries' average	4,0%
Market share of cities > 250,000 inhabitants	29,4%
15 countries' average	42,7%
Portion of competition assessment as "strong" or "very strong"	42,7%
15 countries' average	52,7%
Portion of competition prognosis as "increase" or "strong increase"	76,8%
15 countries' average	81,0%

Offering	
Portion of 1-on-1 training	68,9%
Portion of 1-on-2 training	11,0%
Portion of small group training	20,0%
15 countries' average for 1-on-1 training	72,4%
Price of a 1-on-1 training session (in EUR p.p.)	55
Price of a 1-on-2 training session (in EUR p.p.)	35
Price of a small group training session (in EUR p.p.)	20
15 countries' average for the price of a 1-on-1 training session (in EUR p.p.)	53

Personal Trainer	
Portion female Personal Trainers	37,0%
15 countries' average	36,1%
In absolute numbers	1.506
Average age of Personal Trainers (in years)	37
15 countries' average (in years)	34
Portion of fulltime Personal Trainers	47,8%
15 countries' average	46,3%
In absolute numbers	1.947
Portion of self-employed Personal Trainers	78,3%
15 countries' average	73,1%
In absolute numbers	3.193
Average time spent in industry (in years)	11
15 countries' average (in years)	9
Average time working as Personal Trainer (in years)	6
15 countries' average (in years)	6
Portion of Personal Trainers with a bachelor's degree or higher	36,4%
15 countries' average	32,2%
Portion of "very satisfied" Personal Trainers	43,3%
15 countries' average	37,6%
Average monthly net revenue (in EUR)	2.241
15 countries' average (in EUR)	1.894

Norway

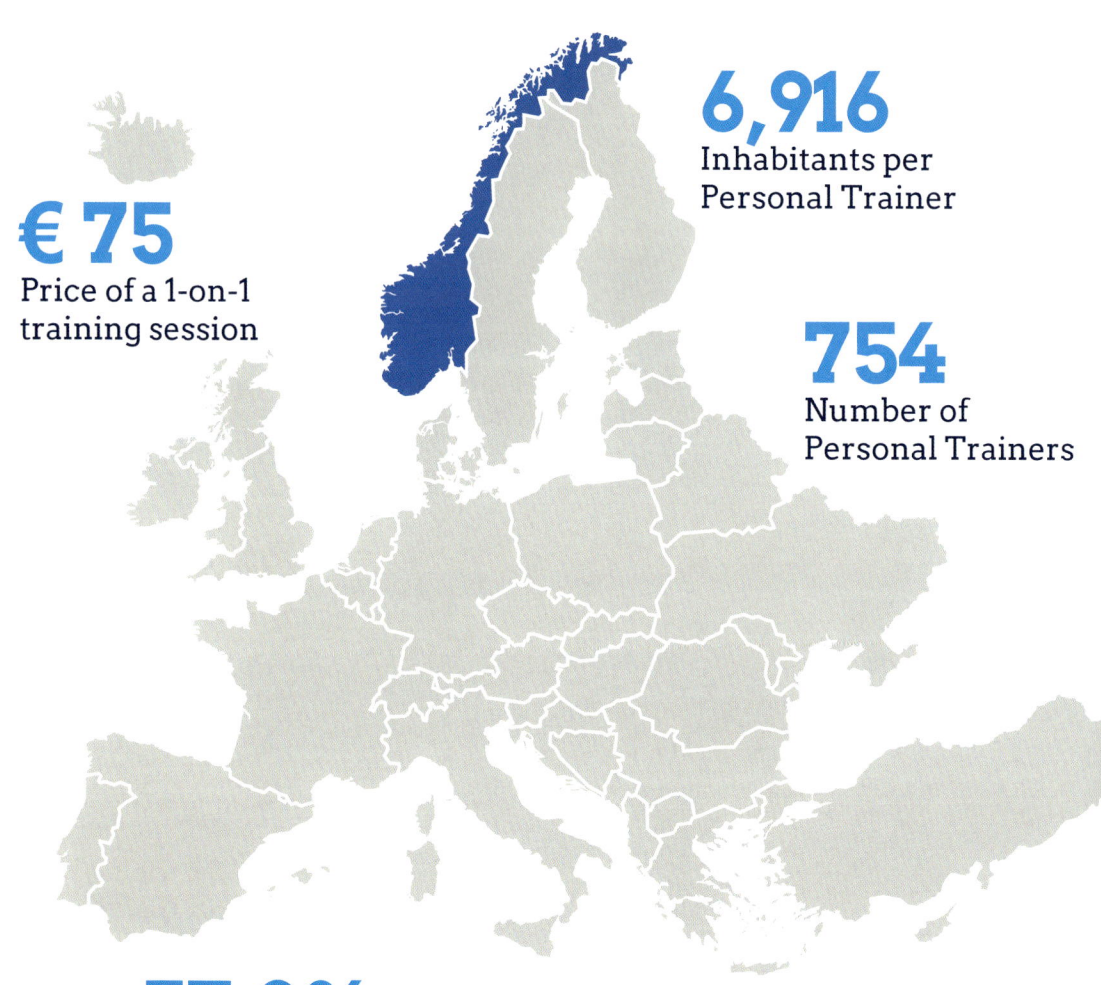

6,916
Inhabitants per Personal Trainer

€ 75
Price of a 1-on-1 training session

754
Number of Personal Trainers

57.8 %
Portion of fulltime Personal Trainers

51.4 %
Portion female Personal Trainers

Personal Training in Europe

General Market Information	
Total general population	5.213.985
Number of Personal Trainers	754
Inhabitants per Personal Trainer	6.916
15 countries' average	5.772
Number of participating Personal Trainers	105
Participation rate	13,9%
15 countries' average	4,0%
Market share of cities > 250,000 inhabitants	45,7%
15 countries' average	42,7%
Portion of competition assessment as "strong" or "very strong"	56,4%
15 countries' average	52,7%
Portion of competition prognosis as "increase" or "strong increase"	70,9%
15 countries' average	81,0%

Offering	
Portion of 1-on-1 training	84,3%
Portion of 1-on-2 training	7,4%
Portion of small group training	8,3%
15 countries' average for 1-on-1 training	72,4%
Price of a 1-on-1 training session (in EUR p.p.)	75
Price of a 1-on-2 training session (in EUR p.p.)	65
Price of a small group training session (in EUR p.p.)	40
15 countries' average for the price of a 1-on-1 training session (in EUR p.p.)	53

Personal Trainer	
Portion female Personal Trainers	51,4%
15 countries' average	36,1%
In absolute numbers	388
Average age of Personal Trainers (in years)	32
15 countries' average (in years)	34
Portion of fulltime Personal Trainers	57,8%
15 countries' average	46,3%
In absolute numbers	436
Portion of self-employed Personal Trainers	36,9%
15 countries' average	73,1%
In absolute numbers	278
Average time spent in industry (in years)	7
15 countries' average (in years)	9
Average time working as Personal Trainer (in years)	5
15 countries' average (in years)	6
Portion of Personal Trainers with a bachelor's degree or higher	33,3%
15 countries' average	32,2%
Portion of "very satisfied" Personal Trainers	27,7%
15 countries' average	37,6%
Average monthly net revenue (in EUR)	2.618
15 countries' average (in EUR)	1.894

Portugal

€ 35
Price of a 1-on-1 training session

2,738
Inhabitants per Personal Trainer

3,777
Number of Personal Trainers

51.8%
Portion of fulltime Personal Trainers

30.5%
Portion female Personal Trainers

Personal Training in Europe

General Market Information	
Total general population	10.341.330
Number of Personal Trainers	3.777
Inhabitants per Personal Trainer	2.738
15 countries' average	5.772
Number of participating Personal Trainers	118
Participation rate	3,1%
15 countries' average	4,0%
Market share of cities > 250,000 inhabitants	42,2%
15 countries' average	42,7%
Portion of competition assessment as "strong" or "very strong"	75,9%
15 countries' average	52,7%
Portion of competition prognosis as "increase" or "strong increase"	93,0%
15 countries' average	81,0%

Offering	
Portion of 1-on-1 training	85,3%
Portion of 1-on-2 training	7,5%
Portion of small group training	7,2%
15 countries' average for 1-on-1 training	72,4%
Price of a 1-on-1 training session (in EUR p.p.)	35
Price of a 1-on-2 training session (in EUR p.p.)	25
Price of a small group training session (in EUR p.p.)	19
15 countries' average for the price of a 1-on-1 training session (in EUR p.p.)	53

Personal Trainer	
Portion female Personal Trainers	30,5%
15 countries' average	36,1%
In absolute numbers	1.152
Average age of Personal Trainers (in years)	34
15 countries' average (in years)	34
Portion of fulltime Personal Trainers	51,8%
15 countries' average	46,3%
In absolute numbers	1.955
Portion of self-employed Personal Trainers	75,4%
15 countries' average	73,1%
In absolute numbers	2.850
Average time spent in industry (in years)	10
15 countries' average (in years)	9
Average time working as Personal Trainer (in years)	7
15 countries' average (in years)	6
Portion of Personal Trainers with a bachelor's degree or higher	76,8%
15 countries' average	32,2%
Portion of "very satisfied" Personal Trainers	22,2%
15 countries' average	37,6%
Average monthly net revenue (in EUR)	1.215
15 countries' average (in EUR)	1.894

Spain

€ 35
Price of a 1-on-1 training session

17,531
Inhabitants per Personal Trainer

2,649
Number of Personal Trainers

38.3%
Portion of fulltime Personal Trainers

25.1%
Portion female Personal Trainers

Personal Training in Europe

General Market Information	
Total general population	46.440.099
Number of Personal Trainers	2.649
Inhabitants per Personal Trainer	17.531
15 countries' average	5.772
Number of participating Personal Trainers	175
Participation rate	6,6%
15 countries' average	4,0%
Market share of cities > 250,000 inhabitants	49,7%
15 countries' average	42,7%
Portion of competition assessment as "strong" or "very strong"	46,3%
15 countries' average	52,7%
Portion of competition prognosis as "increase" or "strong increase"	81,7%
15 countries' average	81,0%

Offering	
Portion of 1-on-1 training	68,5%
Portion of 1-on-2 training	12,6%
Portion of small group training	19,0%
15 countries' average for 1-on-1 training	72,4%
Price of a 1-on-1 training session (in EUR p.p.)	35
Price of a 1-on-2 training session (in EUR p.p.)	25
Price of a small group training session (in EUR p.p.)	19
15 countries' average for the price of a 1-on-1 training session (in EUR p.p.)	53

Personal Trainer	
Portion female Personal Trainers	25,1%
15 countries' average	36,1%
In absolute numbers	666
Average age of Personal Trainers (in years)	35
15 countries' average (in years)	34
Portion of fulltime Personal Trainers	38,3%
15 countries' average	46,3%
In absolute numbers	1.015
Portion of self-employed Personal Trainers	62,7%
15 countries' average	73,1%
In absolute numbers	1.661
Average time spent in industry (in years)	9
15 countries' average (in years)	9
Average time working as Personal Trainer (in years)	6
15 countries' average (in years)	6
Portion of Personal Trainers with a bachelor's degree or higher	46,3%
15 countries' average	32,2%
Portion of "very satisfied" Personal Trainers	37,7%
15 countries' average	37,6%
Average monthly net revenue (in EUR)	1.409
15 countries' average (in EUR)	1.894

Sweden

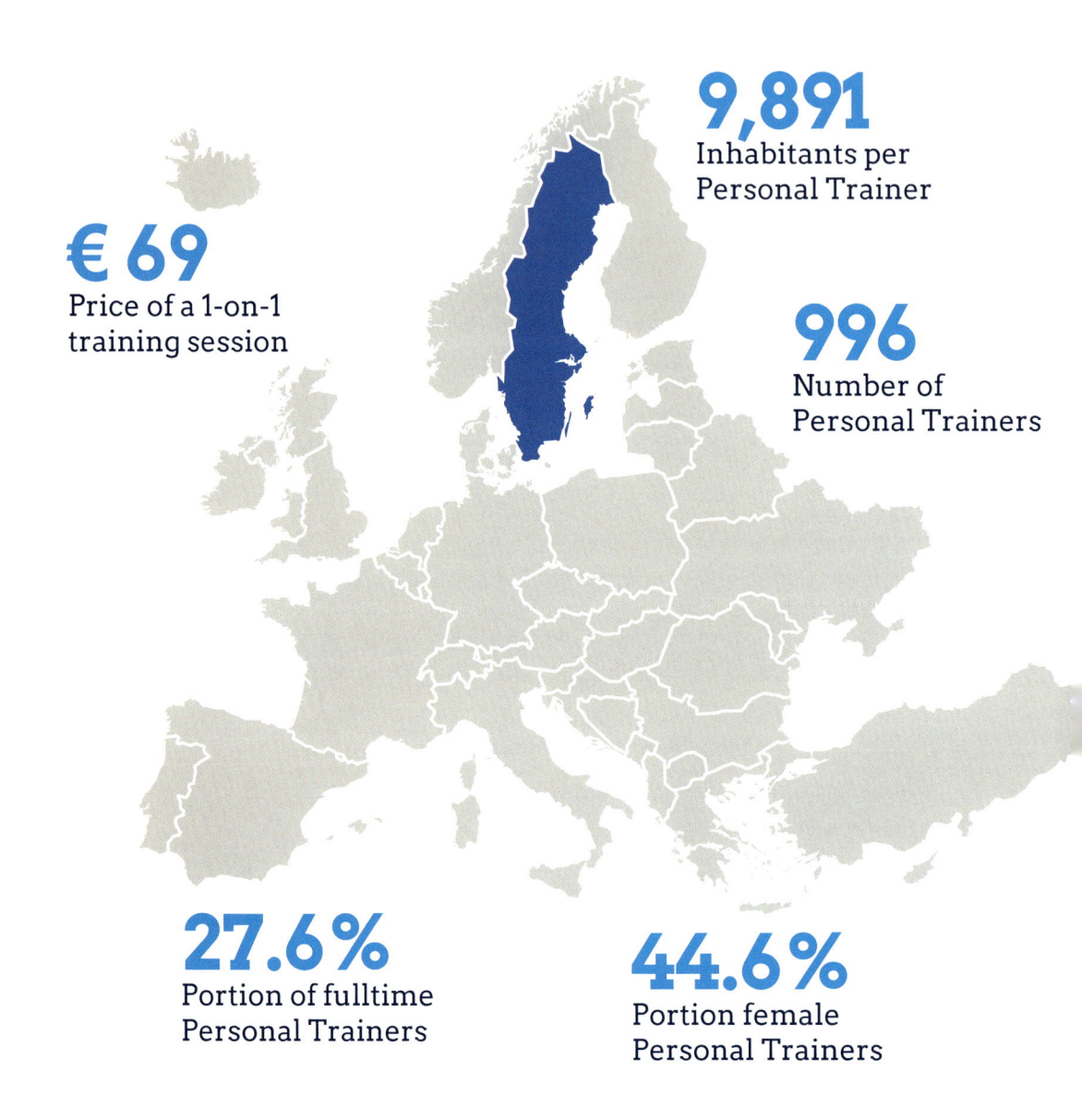

9,891
Inhabitants per Personal Trainer

€ 69
Price of a 1-on-1 training session

996
Number of Personal Trainers

27.6 %
Portion of fulltime Personal Trainers

44.6 %
Portion female Personal Trainers

Personal Training in Europe

General Market Information	
Total general population	9.851.017
Number of Personal Trainers	996
Inhabitants per Personal Trainer	9.891
15 countries' average	5.772
Number of participating Personal Trainers	101
Participation rate	10,1%
15 countries' average	4,0%
Market share of cities > 250,000 inhabitants	43,6%
15 countries' average	42,7%
Portion of competition assessment as "strong" or "very strong"	41,7%
15 countries' average	52,7%
Portion of competition prognosis as "increase" or "strong increase"	75,0%
15 countries' average	81,0%

Offering	
Portion of 1-on-1 training	70,9%
Portion of 1-on-2 training	8,9%
Portion of small group training	20,2%
15 countries' average for 1-on-1 training	72,4%
Price of a 1-on-1 training session (in EUR p.p.)	69
Price of a 1-on-2 training session (in EUR p.p.)	53
Price of a small group training session (in EUR p.p.)	40
15 countries' average for the price of a 1-on-1 training session (in EUR p.p.)	53

Personal Trainer	
Portion female Personal Trainers	44,6%
15 countries' average	36,1%
In absolute numbers	444
Average age of Personal Trainers (in years)	41
15 countries' average (in years)	34
Portion of fulltime Personal Trainers	27,6%
15 countries' average	46,3%
In absolute numbers	274
Portion of self-employed Personal Trainers	50,0%
15 countries' average	73,1%
In absolute numbers	498
Average time spent in industry (in years)	9
15 countries' average (in years)	9
Average time working as Personal Trainer (in years)	6
15 countries' average (in years)	6
Portion of Personal Trainers with a bachelor's degree or higher	13,4%
15 countries' average	32,2%
Portion of "very satisfied" Personal Trainers	31,5%
15 countries' average	37,6%
Average monthly net revenue (in EUR)	1.785
15 countries' average (in EUR)	1.894

Switzerland

€ 119
Price of a 1-on-1 training session

7,160
Inhabitants per Personal Trainer

1,163
Number of Personal Trainers

41.2 %
Portion of fulltime Personal Trainers

41.8 %
Portion female Personal Trainers

Personal Training in Europe

General Market Information	
Total general population	8.327.126
Number of Personal Trainers	1.163
Inhabitants per Personal Trainer	7.160
15 countries' average	5.772
Number of participating Personal Trainers	98
Participation rate	8,4%
15 countries' average	4,0%
Market share of cities > 250,000 inhabitants	29,2%
15 countries' average	42,7%
Portion of competition assessment as "strong" or "very strong"	53,8%
15 countries' average	52,7%
Portion of competition prognosis as "increase" or "strong increase"	88,5%
15 countries' average	81,0%

Offering	
Portion of 1-on-1 training	78,7%
Portion of 1-on-2 training	5,1%
Portion of small group training	16,2%
15 countries' average for 1-on-1 training	72,4%
Price of a 1-on-1 training session (in EUR p.p.)	119
Price of a 1-on-2 training session (in EUR p.p.)	92
Price of a small group training session (in EUR p.p.)	37
15 countries' average for the price of a 1-on-1 training session (in EUR p.p.)	53

Personal Trainer	
Portion female Personal Trainers	41,8%
15 countries' average	36,1%
In absolute numbers	487
Average age of Personal Trainers (in years)	38
15 countries' average (in years)	34
Portion of fulltime Personal Trainers	41,2%
15 countries' average	46,3%
In absolute numbers	480
Portion of self-employed Personal Trainers	74,2%
15 countries' average	73,1%
In absolute numbers	863
Average time spent in industry (in years)	10
15 countries' average (in years)	9
Average time working as Personal Trainer (in years)	7
15 countries' average (in years)	6
Portion of Personal Trainers with a bachelor's degree or higher	27,9%
15 countries' average	32,2%
Portion of "very satisfied" Personal Trainers	55,6%
15 countries' average	37,6%
Average monthly net revenue (in EUR)	3.866
15 countries' average (in EUR)	1.894

United Kingdom

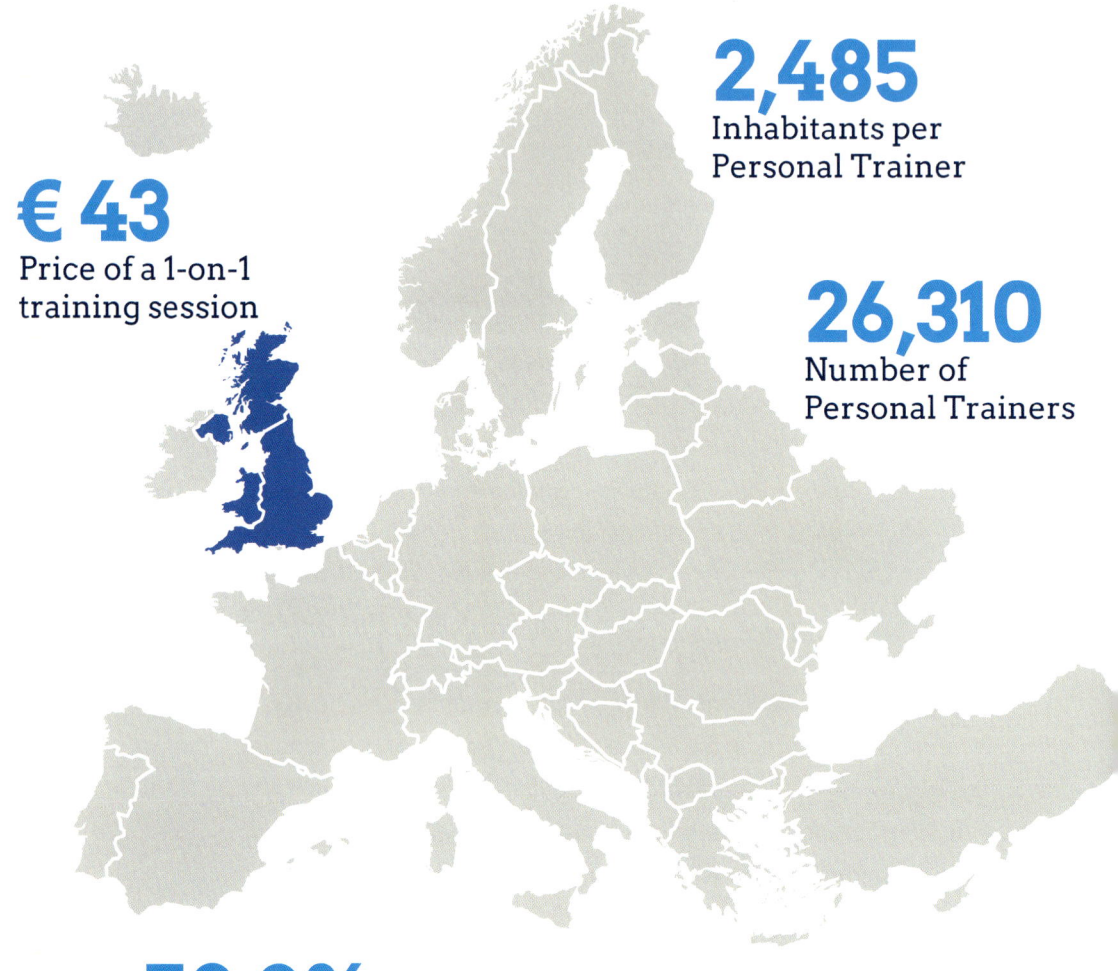

2,485
Inhabitants per Personal Trainer

€ 43
Price of a 1-on-1 training session

26,310
Number of Personal Trainers

58.9%
Portion of fulltime Personal Trainers

36.4%
Portion female Personal Trainers

Personal Training in Europe

General Market Information	
Total general population	65.382.556
Number of Personal Trainers	26.310
Inhabitants per Personal Trainer	2.485
15 countries' average	5.772
Number of participating Personal Trainers	352
Participation rate	1,3%
15 countries' average	4,0%
Market share of cities > 250,000 inhabitants	50,1%
15 countries' average	42,7%
Portion of competition assessment as "strong" or "very strong"	66,2%
15 countries' average	52,7%
Portion of competition prognosis as "increase" or "strong increase"	74,7%
15 countries' average	81,0%

Offering	
Portion of 1-on-1 training	78,7%
Portion of 1-on-2 training	9,8%
Portion of small group training	11,6%
15 countries' average for 1-on-1 training	72,4%
Price of a 1-on-1 training session (in EUR p.p.)	43
Price of a 1-on-2 training session (in EUR p.p.)	31
Price of a small group training session (in EUR p.p.)	18
15 countries' average for the price of a 1-on-1 training session (in EUR p.p.)	53

Personal Trainer	
Portion female Personal Trainers	36,4%
15 countries' average	36,1%
In absolute numbers	9.567
Average age of Personal Trainers (in years)	35
15 countries' average (in years)	34
Portion of fulltime Personal Trainers	58,9%
15 countries' average	46,3%
In absolute numbers	15.494
Portion of self-employed Personal Trainers	82,2%
15 countries' average	73,1%
In absolute numbers	21.631
Average time spent in industry (in years)	8
15 countries' average (in years)	9
Average time working as Personal Trainer (in years)	5
15 countries' average (in years)	6
Portion of Personal Trainers with a bachelor's degree or higher	25,2%
15 countries' average	32,2%
Portion of "very satisfied" Personal Trainers	31,9%
15 countries' average	37,6%
Average monthly net revenue (in EUR)	1.991
15 countries' average (in EUR)	1.894

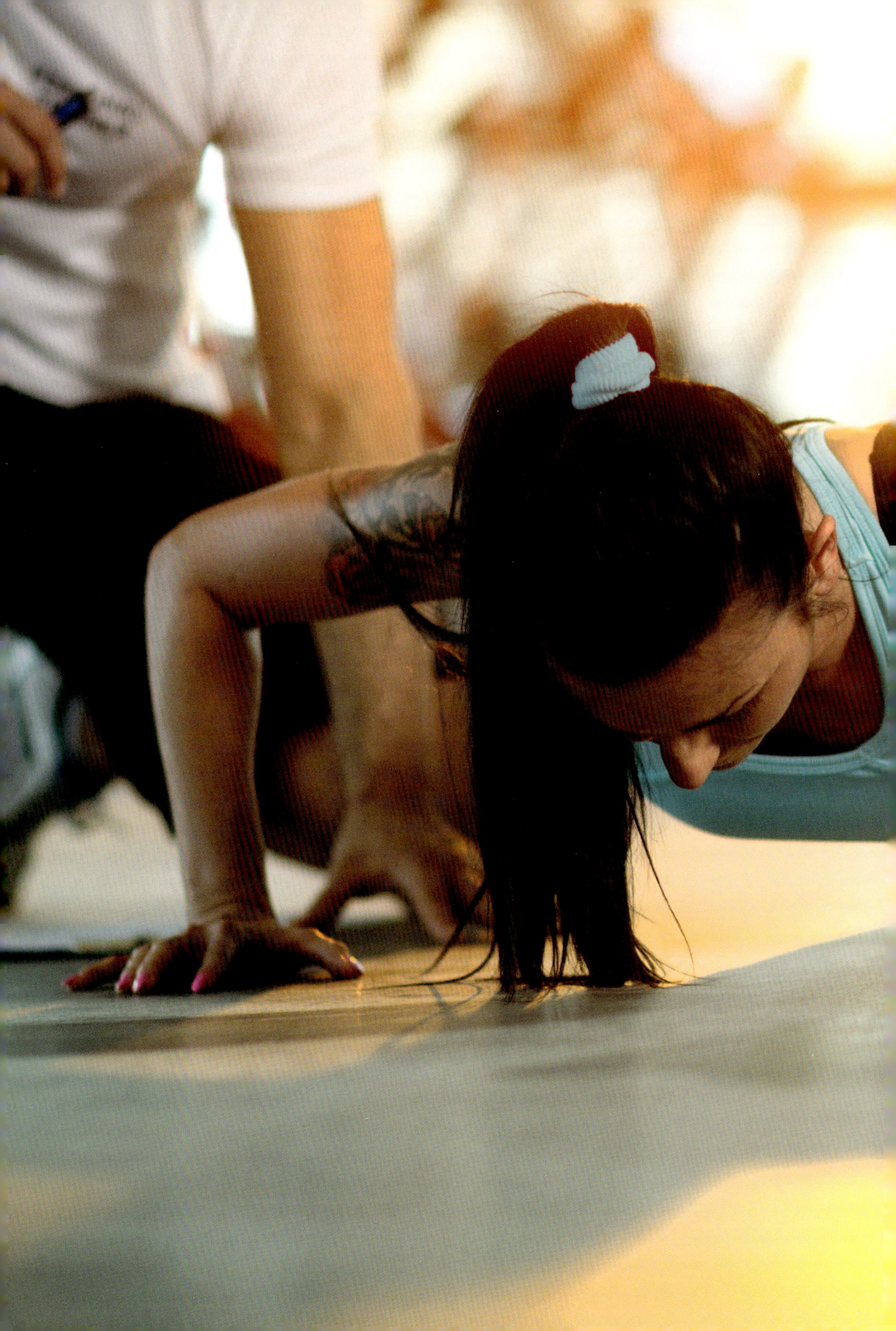

form
4 Perspectives on the Personal Training Market

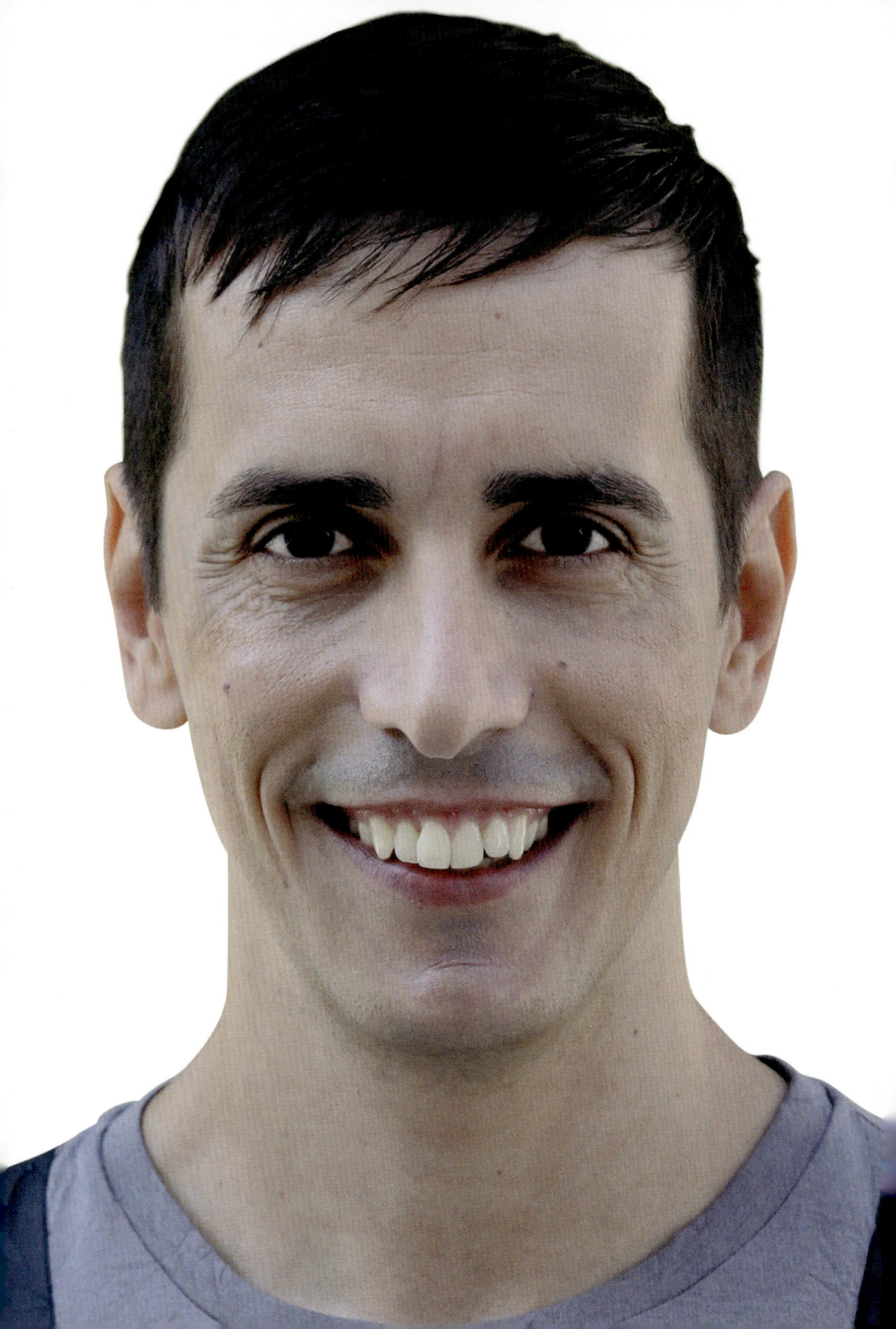

INTERVIEW
Alexis Batrakoulis

Personal Training Education Director

Greek Athletic & Fitness Training School

(GRAFTS)

Alexis Batrakoulis has been involved in the fitness industry since 1995 and currently works as an educator, speaker, author, technical expert, and exercise for health specialist. He is the Personal Training Education Director at the Greek Athletic & Fitness Training School (GRAFTS), which is an accredited vocational training provider and the national leader in fitness certifications in Greece. He holds a BSc in Physical Education and Sports Science with an emphasis on Fitness, an MSc in Exercise and Health with an emphasis on Exercise and Obesity and is preparing to earn a PhD in Exercise and Health.

He has also earned numerous professional credentials through ACE, ACSM, NASM, and NSCA. Alexis is a Subject Matter Expert and an International Master Trainer at the American Council on Exercise (ACE) and is also a member of the Brussels-based Professional Standards Committee of EuropeActive.

How would you basically define Personal Training?

Personal Training has been the top trend in the fitness industry in the last 10 years and so at global level. Trying to define this kind of service is not easy to do, because Personal Training now has many faces compared to the past years. Generally speaking, it is a service that is based on customisation and individualisation of exercise training programmes provided by a qualified fitness professional in different settings (e.g. fitness club, boutique studio, sport club, home, hotel, and outdoor) and through different operational models (e.g. one-on-one, group Personal Training and small-group training sessions).

From your perspective, what are the key factors that influence the demand for Personal Training today and in future?

The fitness industry has always been a rapidly evolving market with a variety of clients, services, facilities, and products. I believe that the need for innovation due to the highly competitive environment within this industry plays a key role. We also know that both high retention and satisfaction rates are crucially associated with the clients' results. Moreover, the current epidemiology statistics regarding the prevalence of many chronic health conditions (i.e. obesity, diabetes, musculoskeletal and cardiovascular disorders etc.) increase the demand for more individualised and high-quality services in our industry. Finally, the economic environment and status in each region is a key factor for the growth of this service and, therefore, it is quite clear that Personal Training is always changing faces in order to be adapted to any circumstances. Thus, the growth of boutique fitness studios worldwide providing mostly small group training sessions using functional training concepts and portable equipment tools is the main outcome of this condition.

How is Personal Training developing in Europe? Would you see it a growth segment within the fitness industry?

Europe is the largest fitness market worldwide with more than 40 countries, which have different characteristics regarding the size, quality level, and penetration rate. In general, the US has always been the leader in the field of Personal Training from many different point of views. The huge difference between the European and the US market is the fact that the first is characterised by serious contrasts regarding the economic situation in each country. At the same time, Personal Training is developing rapidly in Europe and is considered one of the most promising services in our industry for the next years. Actually, a recent survey that was conducted by

EuropeActive and the European Register of Exercise Professionals (EREPS), which I had the honour and opportunity to lead, showed that Personal Trainers and Exercise Specialists would be the most attractive and promising occupational roles for the next 10 years. In terms of my country, Greece is a small market with serious financial issues, but it is following the top global fitness trends and Personal Training is everywhere now nationwide. This comes with a high demand for internationally accredited certification programmes.

What is basically required to be a successful Personal Trainer?

From my point of view, if someone wants to make a difference as Personal Trainer he should focus on many things. But first, the passion and love for this job are some of the most important elements. Every Personal Trainer should want to support clients to make a behaviour change, help them change their lives. To do that, the Personal Trainer should play the role of a mentor, a counsellor, and a coach – and not only the role of an instructor.

More than that, candidates need a comprehensive education and certification in the field of exercise science and Personal Training, respectively. In addition, the continuing education is a key element for the Personal Trainers who seek to stay updated and competitive trying to bridge the gap between theory and practice. Finally, all the top Personal Trainers worldwide invest in soft skills (social and communication skills) that can make a serious difference because these seem to be the most underestimated skills in the profile of a fitness professional.

For you as a training provider, what are the current topics that are demanded the most or that you would particularly recommend Personal Trainers to acquire?

As a Fitness Educator in Greece and worldwide, I strongly believe that the future in the Personal Training field is highly associated with the knowledge and skills related to the supervision and instruction of special populations struggling with controlled health conditions. Just look at the epidemiology statistics and understand the health history and profile of the average client nowadays. In developed countries, almost 50% of adults are physically inactive and have at least one or two risk factors for the development of cardiometabolic diseases (e.g. obesity, type 2 diabetes, hypertension, dyslipidemia, metabolic syndrome, or coronary heart disease). Actually, I can feel that the time that medical community and fitness industry will be working together for the individuals who want to have a healthier, fitter, and happier life will be reality in the future under the umbrella of exercise referral. Therefore,

Personal Trainers who believe that exercise is the best medicine will be able to do the next big step in their careers by working closer together with allied health professionals as a key member of a multidisciplinary healthcare team.

From your personal experience, which role do technical aids of any kind already play in the field of Personal Training? How will the importance of these technical side develop in future?

It is a real fact that technology is one of the key factors why the fitness industry is developing and evolving so fast! According to the latest findings of a survey that was conducted by the American College of Sports Medicine (ACSM) concerning the top worldwide fitness trends in our industry for this year, 3 out of 20 trends in that list are associated with the use of technology (e.g. wearable technology, smartphone exercise apps, and outcome measurements). Additionally, I believe that all the devices that can provide tools for behaviour change (i.e. steps count data daily), individualised exercise intensity (i.e. heart rate monitoring), time-effective training modalities (i.e. EMS) and innovative workouts (i.e. virtual training programmes) will play an important role within the health and fitness industry in the future.

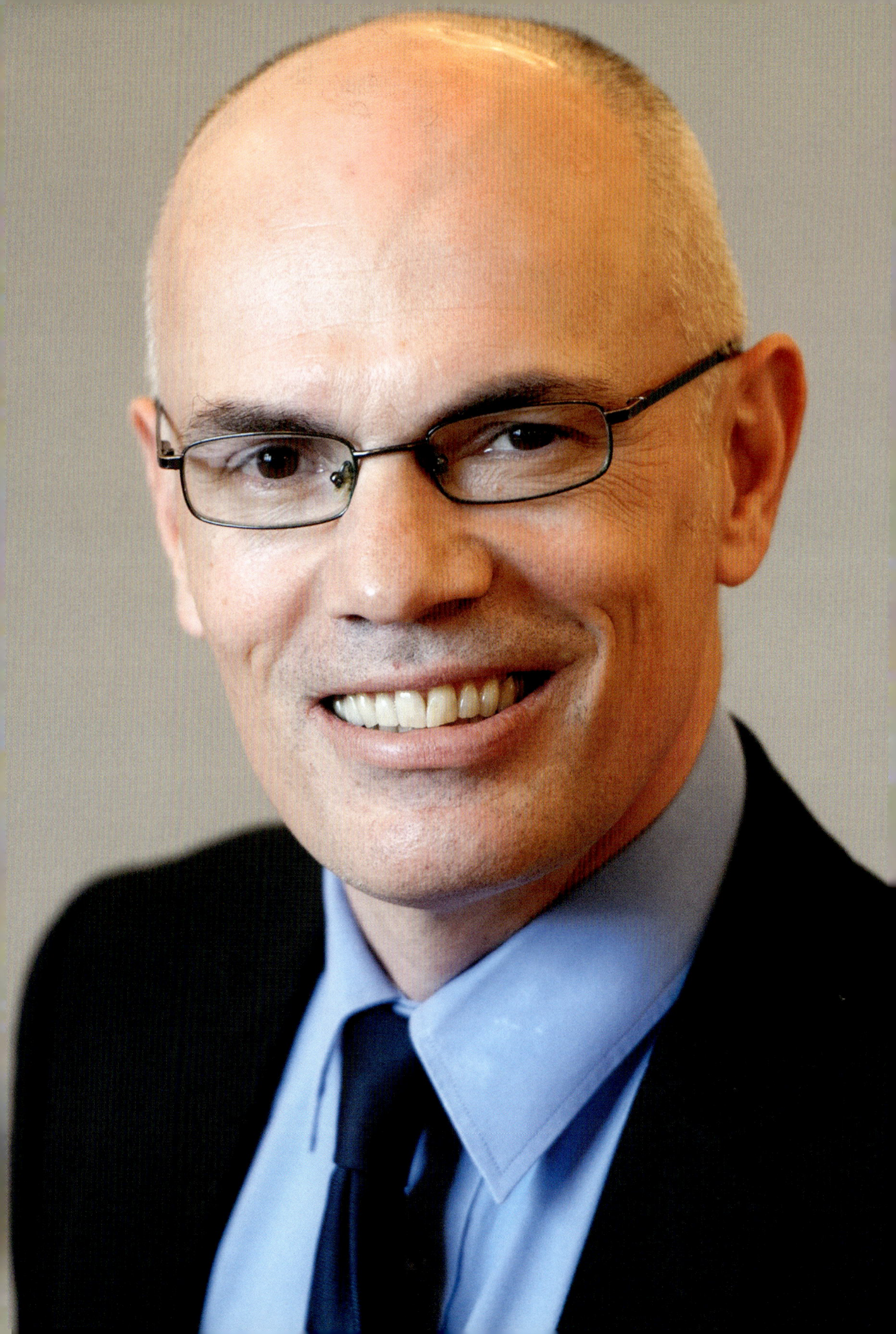

INTERVIEW
Julian Berriman

Director Professional Standards Committee

EuropeActive

Julian Berriman MA, BSc (Hons) Ost is the Director of EuropeActive's Professional Standards Committee with responsibility for overseeing the development and review of EuropeActive's Sector Qualifications Framework. These educational standards have been developed in wide consultation with the European fitness industry and are the basis for the accreditation of training providers and individual instructors and trainers across Europe, as part of the European Register of Exercise Professionals. He has worked within the fitness sector in the UK for more than 20 years and has directed both an industry-leading training provider and awarding organisation. Within these roles he has written, delivered and managed vocational qualifications at all levels.

Outside of his work with EuropeActive Mr. Berriman is a Registered Osteopath and integrates his knowledge of Personal Training with his osteopathic practice.

How would you personally define Personal Training?

I would always have to refer to the EuropeActive educational standards in defining any job role within the fitness sector. Within the EuropeActive Level 4 Personal Trainer standards the job purpose of a Personal Trainer is defined as coaching clients individually according to their fitness needs, through a coordinated exercise/physical activity plan and assisting with behavioural change. This definition has been agreed through widespread consultation with experts and key stakeholders from across the European fitness industry.

EuropeActive's standards also define a Personal Trainer's role. This role includes designing, implementing, and evaluating exercise/physical activity programmes for apparently healthy and low risk adult populations by collecting and analysing client information to ensure the effectiveness of personal exercise programmes. A Personal Trainer should also actively encourage potential clients/members to participate in and adhere to regular exercise/physical activity programmes, employing appropriate motivational strategies to achieve this.

This role is increasingly applied in different settings including the gym, client's homes or outdoors and in both one-to one and small group situations.

From your perspective, what are the key factors that influence the demand for Personal Training today and in future?

According to EuropeActive's Deloitte Market Report 2017, the European fitness sector is growing at an impressive rate of 4% per year. Fitness is the largest participation sport and the only sector in the wider sports sector that has shown an increase in participation. The rise of fitness and the industry's growth must ultimately positively influence the demand for Personal Training. However, this will only happen if the Personal Trainer possesses the right skills to meet future demands.

The World Health Organisation (2013) estimates that a quarter of European adults, and four-fifths of European adolescents, are insufficiently active. This may be the result of changing job roles and technological innovation however; the health consequences of such sedentary lifestyles are significant. The non-communicable diseases associated with inactivity also impose immense economic costs. Add to this blight of inactivity the fact that the proportion of people of working age in the EU is shrinking while the relative number of those retired is expanding and we have a clear picture of an increasingly inactive and elderly population with dire social and economic costs.

Penetration rates (fitness club members in percent of total population - EuropeActive, Deloitte 2017 Report) vary considerably across Europe from 21% to 7%. But if we as an industry and Personal Trainers are to increase these penetration rates and the level of demand for their services they will need the know-how and skills to be confident, able, and trusted to deal with the inactive, the unwell, and the ageing. If the occupation of Personal Training can elevate itself to this degree through thorough and high-quality training supported by relevant and suitably rewarded employment opportunities, then in terms of growth figures we will truly excel!

How is Personal Training developing in Europe? Would you see it a growth segment within the fitness industry?

Certainly, as the wider industry continues to grow across Europe I would consider Personal Training as a growth segment but as an occupation it will need to continue to adapt and develop. We all know that in terms of ill-health prevention is always better than cure and Personal Trainers can be part of the preventative solution. They can partner with other healthcare professions in offering positive health interventions, but this will only happen if those healthcare professions perceive that we have the necessary skills and professional competences to meet the challenge. There is unfortunately a credibility gap where medical professionals do not perceive the quality of training and on-going professional development that gives them the confidence to refer to us or work alongside us. EuropeActive and the European Register of Exercise Professionals (EREPS) can lead the drive to further professionalise our sector in the development of higher level training such as the one required by our Level 5 Exercise for Health Specialist standards, but we will need the buy in and support of training providers, employers and other key industry stakeholders in consolidating vocational solutions that will be widely accepted and implemented.

What is basically required to be a successful Personal Trainer?

Over the years I have trained and assessed many aspiring Personal Trainers and watched high level trainers at work. I think the common ingredients for the high level Personal Trainer are an absolute passion for their work, a real attention to detail in meeting their client's needs and, above all else, an ability to establish a rapport with each and every client. There is no 'one size fits all' in terms of communication but the exceptional Personal Trainer is able to attune themselves to the personality type and needs of their client in order to make sessions motivating, inspiring, and fun. It is no coincidence that these Personal Trainers have also invested in high quality training and are driven to continue to develop and grow as a professional through taking part in an on-going programme of continuing education. I sincerely hope that EuropeActive and EREPS are able to play a significant part in facilitating this career development through the EREPS Lifelong Learning Programme which requires members to commit to an annual programme of continuing education and reflective practice.

For you as a training provider, what are the current topics that are demanded the most or that you would particularly recommend Personal Trainers to acquire?

We have recently reviewed and updated EuropeActive's L4 Personal Training standards in consultation with experts across the industry. There have been a number of minor amendments, but the key additions have been to strengthen the existing standards relating to communication skills and the inclusion of aspects relating to business/marketing skills. I think these inclusions reflect a recognition of the fact that Personal Training is not simply about technical knowledge of how the body works and responds to exercise and technical skills related to programme design and implementation. The ability to relate to clients, to establish a rapport and to empathise with them are key skills which have at times been overlooked. These skills become particularly important when attempting to engage with an inactive population who may feel detached and alienated by an industry which has over-focused on striving for physical aesthetics rather than on the joy of physical activity and the sense of well-being it can confer.

To be successful the Personal Trainer must also possess entrepreneurial skills and be able to attract clients through appropriate sales skills. They must see that getting and keeping clients is not about the hard sell but instead utilising their ability to communicate and empathise with clients to attract and continually motivate clients.

I have already mentioned the importance of being able to work with those with one or more non-communicable diseases or co-morbidities. This will require the Personal Trainer to take on higher level knowledge and skills including the ability to converse and work with health care workers in a highly professional and clinically-led environment.

From your personal experience, which role do technical aids of any kind already play in the field of Personal Training already? How will the importance of these technical side develop in future?

The recent update of the Level 4 Personal Trainer EuropeActive standards also included additional content in the use of appropriate technological developments. This content covers how technological innovations such as heart rate monitors, wearables, and mobile phone applications can engage and support clients in maintaining recommended physical activity levels.

Being able to work with new technologies will become increasingly important. Personal Trainers must fully understand the advantages but also the limitations of wearable technology or food/fitness app trackers on modern devices in order to fully exploit these tools to create client motivation and adherence.

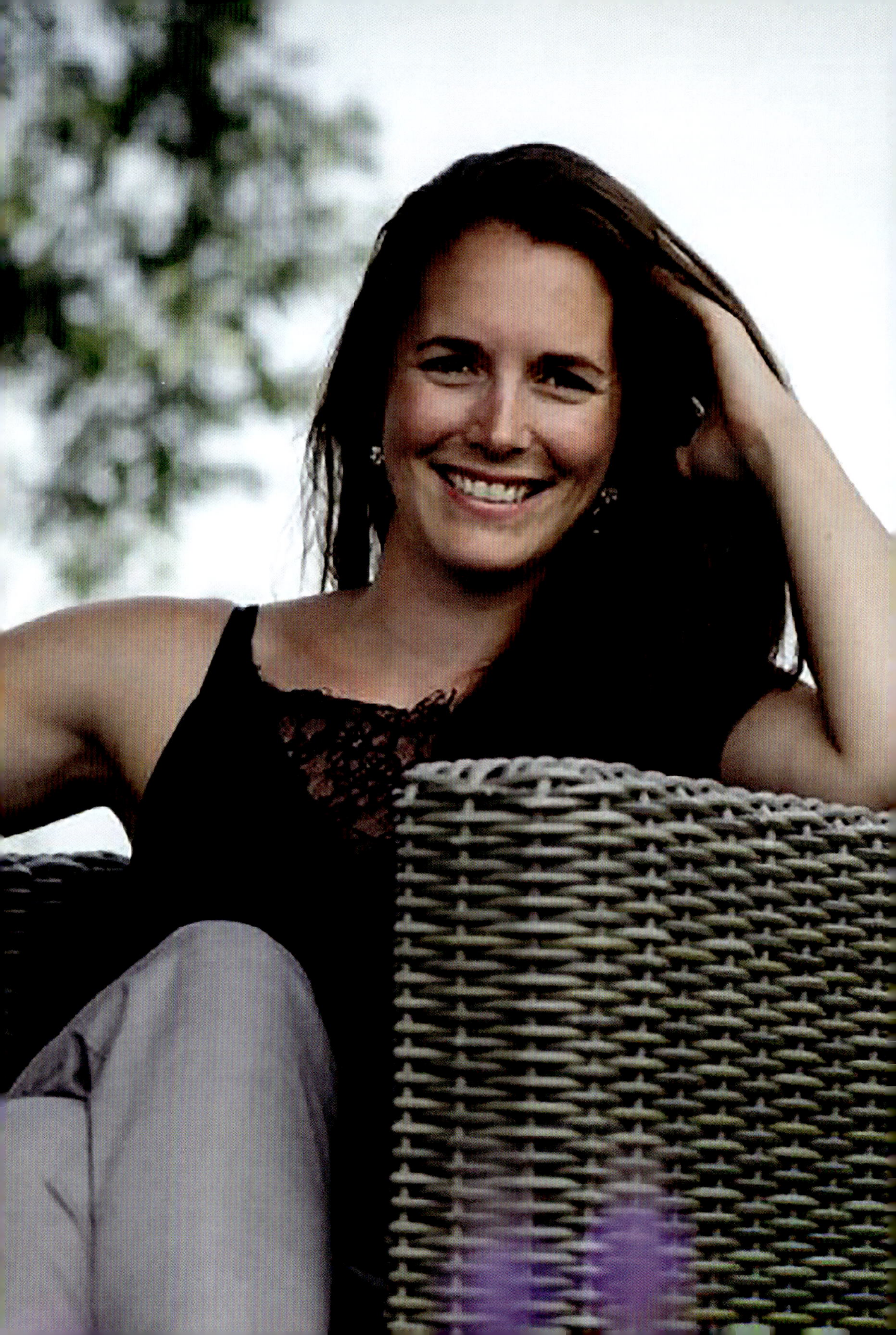

INTERVIEW
Kelby Jongen

International Personal Training Consultant

Co-Owner BlackBoxPublishers and Sport&People (Fitness Educations)

Kelby Jongen has a degree in exercise programming and sports management. She started as a Personal Trainer in 2006 and was the National Personal Training Manager at Fitness First (a chain of 57 clubs in The Benelux). Later she became the International Personal Training and Group Fitness Manager for HealthCity/ BasicFit (a chain of 350 clubs in Europe).

In the meantime, she opened her own Personal Training Studio, named BodyChange, with ten Personal Trainers servicing 350 clients. Kelby was the TV trainer for Obese in The Netherlands and is a key educator for multiple training providers. She published two books, is co-owner of BlackBoxPublishers, the publishing partner of EuropeActive, and co-owner of Sport&People, a government recognised fitness training provider.

How would you personally define Personal Training?

According to my definition, training and small group training is still "personal" with a maximum of six clients. A Personal Trainer needs specific skills to execute for example small group training sessions. Personal Training starts with an assessment to scan what is possible for the client and to explore where possible dysfunctions exist.

In the beginning, a comprehensive examination gives me a lot of information on how to help the client in all kinds of lifestyle-related habits. Important for me is to go the extra mile for my client. They pay a lot for the Personal Training service, so it needs to be very personal, complete, and a pleasant experience.

From your perspective, what are the key factors that influence the demand for Personal Training today and in future?

Many Personal Trainers focus on the same goals such as weight loss, gaining muscles, and getting fitter. But for the future, Personal Trainers need to choose more specific target groups. And they have to create unique selling points. It would be fantastic to see an increase in level 5 trainers, more specialists and a better image of the Personal Trainer profession. This would be very helpful when working in cooperation with physiotherapists or doctors. Currently, it is unclear (to potential customers and other professions) what Personal Trainers are doing.

When specific programs are paid by insurance companies, the group of Personal Training clients will grow. But I'm not sure whether this is a good prospect for the business of the Personal Trainer. The price could drop.

How is Personal Training developing in Europe? Would you see it a growth segment within the fitness industry? What is its potential?

It grows fast in Holland. According to a recent study, The Netherlands counts a total of 623 Personal Training studios, with approximately 50% of them opening in the last three years. The profession of Personal Trainers has very low entrance levels, so everybody can just become a Personal Trainer.

For me, it is a long-term mission that this will stop. The sooner the better. The basic education for starting as fitness professional needs to be raised to a higher level. In sum, there is a lot of potential, but we have to work hard to increase the quality of trainers.

What is basically required to be a successful Personal Trainer? What are the key characteristics someone needs to have or acquire to work in this field?

The personal character in combination with specialism is the key to success. You can be a trainer with a long list of certifications but when your character does not match with the client it does not work in the long run. A Personal Trainer goes the extra mile, is friendly, is a role model, thinks high end, and is a professional; and of course, has the right certifications. The trainer should be open-minded and embrace life-long learning.

With respect to current trends, what are the upcoming topics for Personal Training one should definitely follow up with?

We need more focus on lifestyle coaching in general. Exercise is a fantastic medicine, but a difficult big habit to many clients.
So, we also need to focus on tiny habits in daily live; to coach the clients to create their own nutrition plan, give the clients knowledge about sleep, stress, and movement in daily live to really help the clients to a better live and a long-term success. In the end, however, the clients must do it by themselves.

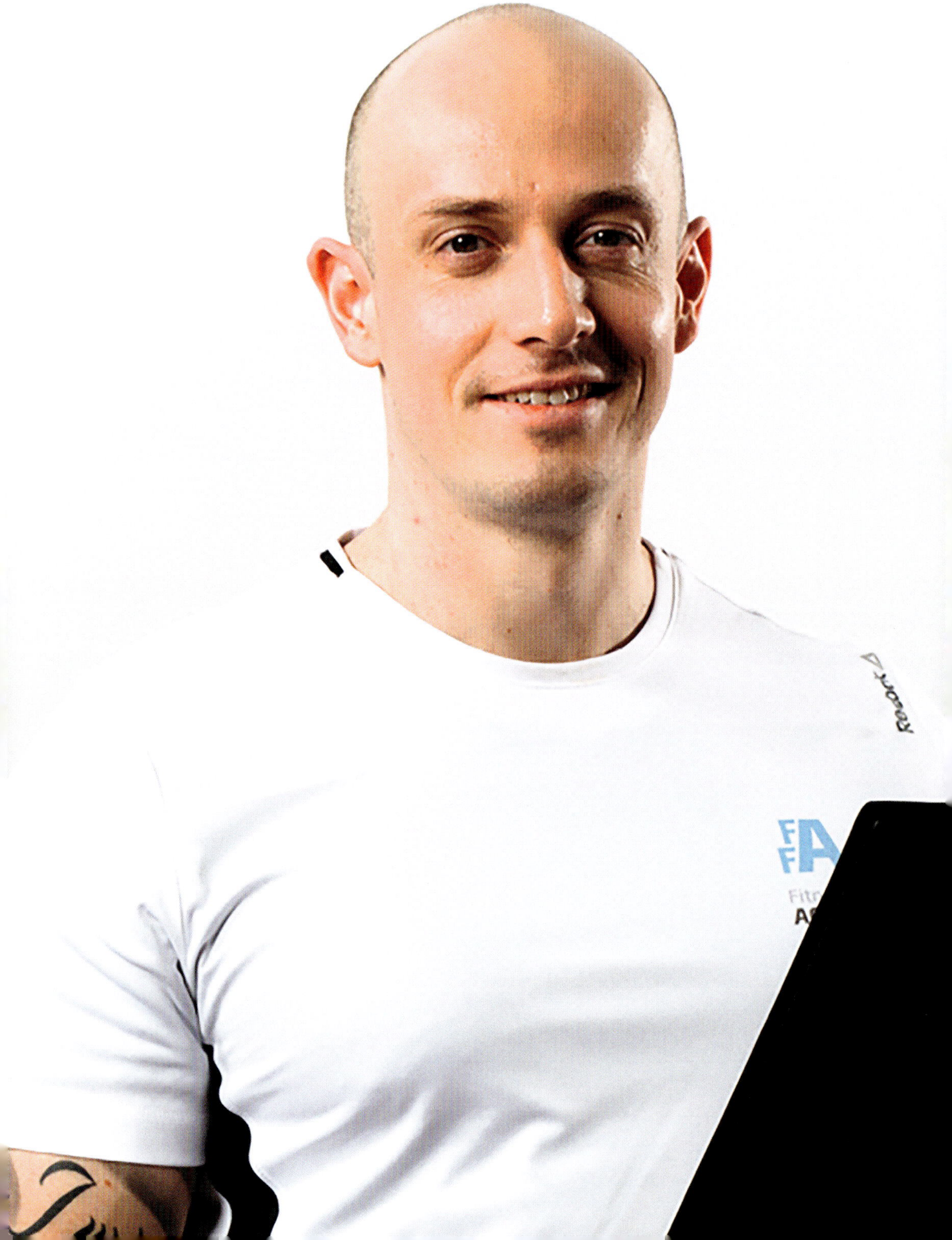

INTERVIEW
Sascha Linz

Manager Fitness First

Academy

Fitness First Germany

Sascha Linz is a self-employed Personal Trainer since 2006 until now. He as earned a Bachelor of Arts degree in Fitness Economics and a Master of Arts in Health Care Management. He has worked in different roles at Fitness First in Germany. Amongst others as club manager and cluster club manager, Personal Training and fitness manager and Personal Training coordinator. Since 2017 he is manager of the newly established Fitness First Academy. Beyond that he is active as speaker for learning and training in the field of health and fitness.

How would you basically define Personal Training?

I define Personal Training as an individual planned, guided, executed, and evaluated form of exercise prescription including exclusive customer service, surveillance, and recommendations, all focused on achieving the client's training goal(s). Originally, Personal Training used to be executed 1-on-1. There are many reasons for this such as ensuring that the client receives 100% attention from the trainer and 100% alignment to his individual goals. Nevertheless, 1-on-2 or small group training can be a proper alternative for people who can't afford the money for 1-on-1 or want to train together in a group or team — as long as they have roughly the same goals. Otherwise, the outcome for everyone can be pretty much different and no one achieves their personal goals. But because many different types and ways of Personal Training exist in practice and because it is also not clear what is actually meant by the term 'Personal Training' the opinions may differ in that point.

From your perspective, what are the key factors that influence the demand for Personal Training today and in future?

In my opinion there are a lot of key factors and they are developing day by day and year by year. But first of all, we should go back shortly to question 1 what Personal Training actually should be because there exist different methods in different countries or even in different companies. While in some countries or companies the word ´Personal Trainer` is just the synonym for every member of the fitness team that offers free training support for the customers, in other countries or companies the Personal Trainer is a synonym for a way higher educated and specialised fitness expert who deals with clients that have certain specific needs and these trainers have to be booked and payed on top to the monthly membership fee. In the further course I will refer to the last understanding of Personal Trainers.

The key factors that influence the demand for Personal Training today are the result of the changes in our work environment and the fact that employees – compared to the past – sit way more, walk way less, eat worse, do way less hard body work, do way more screen work (computer, tablets etc.) which all leads to lower muscle activation, overweight, worse posture and way more physical and mental stress. Employees need to adjust their work-life-balance and fitness training and especially Personal Training can reduce all of these negative influences and re-energize to keep on working by having a solid physical and mental base.

Of course, there are other types of Personal Training clients such as athletes, but these are definitely in the minority compared to the huge number of Personal Trainers out there. Having a look into the future, I think these influences will still exist for a long time – but watch out: there will be even more… such as digitalization that will maybe aggravate the behaviour of people mentioned above.

How is Personal Training developing in Europe? Would you see it a growth segment within the fitness industry? What is its potential?

It is definitely developing. The number of self-employed or employed Personal Trainers is growing. Depending on the country there are differences in the form of development and also of work status and delivered quality. In Germany, the majority in the Personal Training Business is still self-employed but the number of employed Personal Trainers is growing day by day – of course also influenced by the big fitness chains who began a few years ago and still continue to hire more employed Personal Trainers to secure the member service and to offer additional products to their customers. Compared to the US the German market is not growing that fast but its growing consistently. In my opinion there is even a bigger potential in Germany than yet realised but it is important to deliver high quality to the customers. To ensure this the Personal Trainers have to be very well educated and also updated to science, customer care, excellent service focus etc.

We at Fitness First ensure this for example by our own Fitness First Academy that is not just for internal usage but also for everyone who wants to be educated and certified in a high qualified way with chances to find a proper employed or self-employed Personal Trainer job afterwards either at Fitness First Germany or anywhere else.

What is basically required to be a successful Personal Trainer?

The base is definitely a high quality fundamental education combined with a high level of certification. This should include all the scientific knowledge that is needed plus skills in assessment, training planning, training surveillance and evaluation. But even if it is the requirement this base is just 20% responsible for having success as a Personal Trainer. But what is way more important is to catch the emotional level of your client. Your intercommunication has to be good, they must see you as a kind of idol, they need the impression and feeling that you are the one that will lead them to their individual and specific goals. Of course, spreading fun and the implementation of a new life behaviour in the client's mind are also very important. All together the soft skills are 80% responsible whether the Personal Trainer will be successful or not. The better the 20% of training education and the goal achievement of the clients are, the more long-term success will the Personal Trainer have. What should not be worth talking about is the neat appearance of the trainer and that he is on time at every appointment with his customers.

For you as a training provider, what are the current topics that are demanded the most or that you would particularly recommend Personal Trainers to acquire?

It all starts with the fundamental science base of knowledge. In my opinion the most important thing is to ensure that the education base is solid, and the training knowledge of the Personal Trainer is up to date. So, the Personal Trainer should only participate at accredited training providers to get a high-quality education. The Fitness First Academy is accredited by EuropeActive and participates every two years in a re-accreditation to proof the high quality in processes and scientific content. On top the quality management of our academy is approved and certified by the German quality norm DIN ISO 9001:2015. At Fitness First Academy you start with a so-called Fitness-Trainer-B-License (EQF Level 3) to set the base and to be able to deal with general issues and goals of fitness club members followed by the Fitness-Trainer-A-License (EQF Level 4) which deals with specific topics, teaches the whole job and techniques of a Personal Trainer and even the setup of an own self-employed Personal Training business (for more information please visit us at: ff-academy.de).

So, I recommend Personal Trainers a holistic training education that puts them into a position that they feel safe and comfortable in front of their clients and that they are able to deal with all the issues the situation demands. To stabilise and develop the trainer's knowledge they should participate every year at least at one or better at several 1-day or 2-daysworkshops on certain topics the market demands (such as product innovations, special equipment, new testing methods etc....) In the last decade there has been a huge change among German providers, so today every training provider offers also 1-day, 2-day or short education forms to be attractive also for people who like to enter the fitness industry or even just want to improve their own knowledge because they are passionate fitness consumers without having interest in being a fitness profession.

From your personal experience, which role do technical aids of any kind play in the field of Personal Training? How will the importance of these technical side develop in future?

The market of technical aids is growing and there is already a big market existing out there. But we have to differentiate the consideration of technical aids in tracking aids and organization aids. If we consider the tracking aids you still find complicated handlings, a lot of manual input is needed, and technical links are missing to connect for example different kinds of apps properly. Besides that, the apps are also not able to give you feedback whether your exercise movement is correct or will not motivate you in the way a Personal Trainer can do in a live session. Considering organization aids there are already a few good ones out there that can support the personal organization of a food diary, amount and status quo of training and training results and especially the possibility of online bookings for certain issues is a meaningful improvement.

To come to the conclusion, the new technical aids can be seen as an additional help in some way but technical aids will never replace a real trainer that can react by his senses and not just by data that is put into a computer or app. But it can be sometimes a good start for people to deal with the topic and maybe help to find the courage to take the next step – to consult a professional Personal Trainer. In my opinion the technical aids need to be developed better to reign in the market and get even more influence on the fitness consumers. But the first step is done – let's have a look what the future will bring!

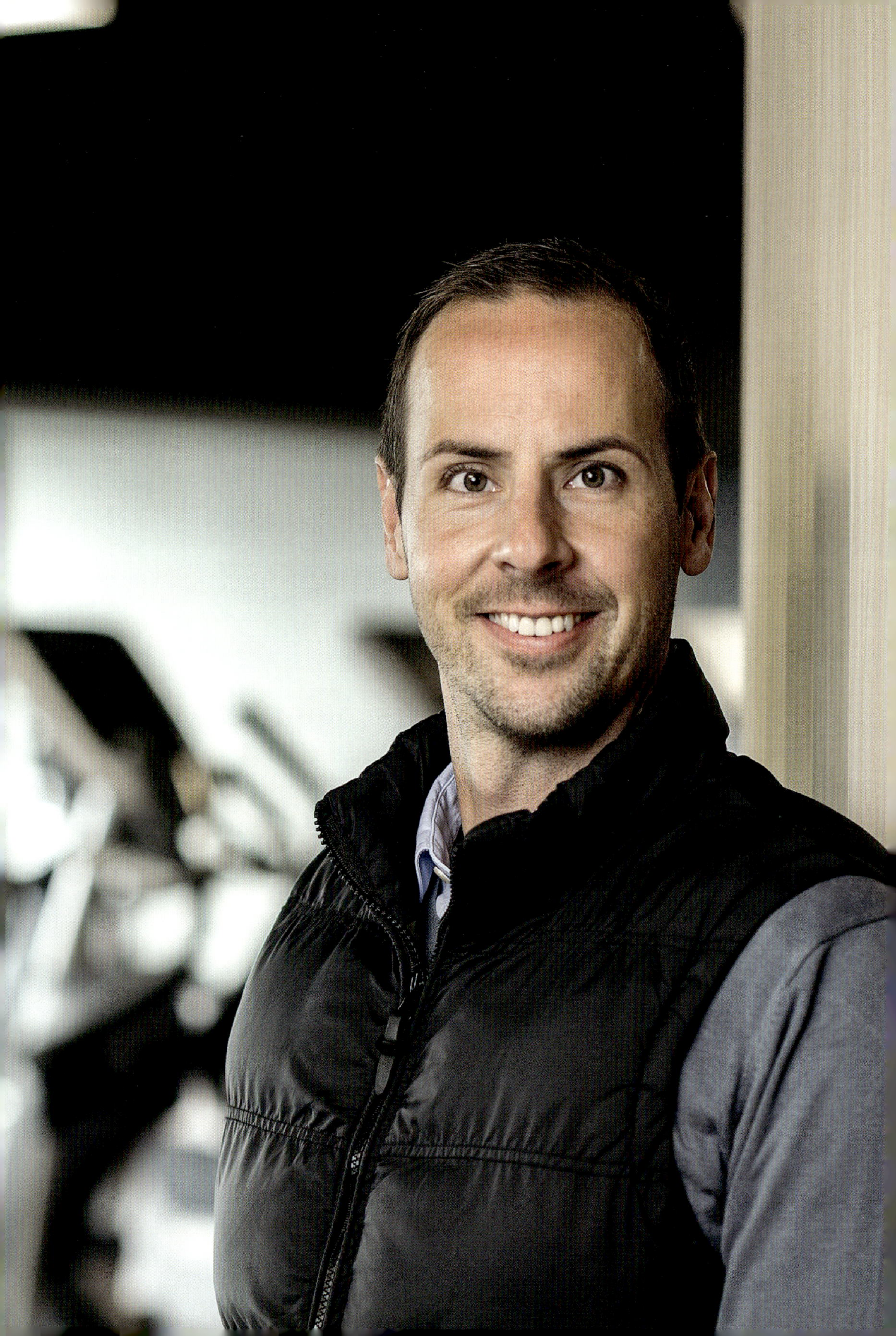

INTERVIEW
Helko Roth

Head of Marketing and Business Development

Migros Aare cooperative

Helko Roth has been involved with the international fitness market for more than 10 years. Following on from a course of studies with the emphasis on marketing, he continued his education in the fields of business development, coaching & process support. In his current position as Head of Marketing and Business Development Leisure, he is responsible both for business development and the marketing of various fitness brands within the Migros Aare cooperative.

From your perspective, what are the key factors that influence the demand for Personal Training today and in future?

In my opinion, one of the main drivers for Personal Training is the high level of time flexibility in an age of heavy workloads, often accompanied by a lack of time. In addition, the desire for one-to-one support is also an important factor. This support often focusses on exercise and, where appropriate, nutrition. While the focus today is heavily oriented towards the customer's activity and, where appropriate, their nutritional profile, further customer factors will become relevant in the future. One example that could be mentioned here is the integration of the customer's sleep analysis. I think that this might lead to much greater integration of the Personal Trainer in the customer's life. What makes this possible is the progressive digitalisation in all areas of life. Moreover, this development also makes it possible to provide remote customer support at times. We are also already seeing complementary customer support today using digital tracking. This offers a means of meeting a demand, particularly at a time of increasing mobility.

How is Personal Training developing in Europe / your country? Would you see it a growth segment within the fitness industry? What is its potential?

In contrast to the Anglo-Saxon countries, training support in Central Europe was commonly part and parcel of a fitness membership. Especially so in the higher price segment. This has changed to some extent in recent years as a consequence of the strong growth in the lower price segment. Because of their structure, these "big box" concepts also provide very little or no personal support. I can therefore well imagine that this might lead to a trend towards "double membership". That is to say, customers will not only be consumers of Personal Training but also have a fitness studio membership at the same time since these are increasingly seen as social meeting points. All in all, therefore, I anticipate the Personal Trainer market to continue to develop positively in future.

How do you integrate Personal Training in your club and other operations from an organizational perspective? What is the specific model your Personal Trainers work in?

At Migros Aare, we work exclusively with employed Personal Trainers. Here, the Personal Trainers are attached to a particular club, but can also be deployed to other clubs should the need arise. This organisation is complemented with a central area manager. This person is responsible for the ongoing development of the Migros Aare Personal Trainer concept known as "My Personaltraining".

"My Personaltraining" governs, among other things, the requirements placed on the trainers and the infrastructure, the offering and the administrative processes as well as pricing and thus forms the framework for the day-to-day work of our Personal Trainers.

What are the selection criteria you use in choosing the right people to work as a Personal Trainer in your company? Could you rate specific characteristics or experiences in their meaning?

The term Personal Trainer is not protected in Switzerland and, thus, not subject to any uniform standards. Migros Aare has therefore created its own professional requirements profile for basic and advanced training which is also implemented in consultation with the Swiss Association of Personal Trainers. Applicants wishing to be employed by us as a Personal Trainer must have at least completed a federally recognised course of training as a fitness instructor. In addition, we also check that our Personal Trainers have the appropriate social skills, which is indispensable for work of this kind with customers. Following on from this, they undergo a basic in-house training that depicts our customers' needs and requirements. An integral part of our "My Personaltraining" concept is on-going training of the Personal Trainers and the mutual exchange of experience that takes place at least twice a year.

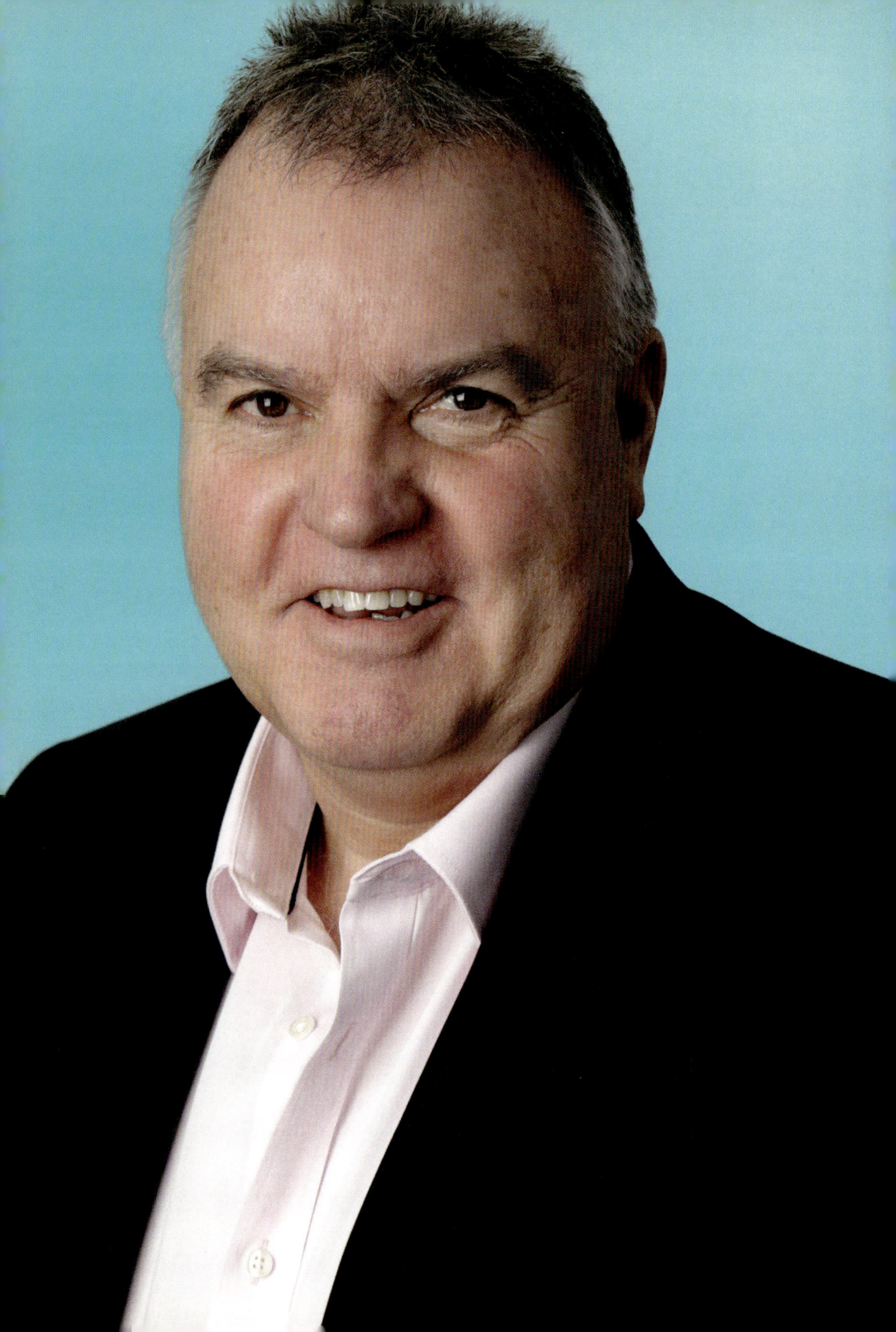

INTERVIEW
John Treharne

Chief Executive Officer

The Gym Group

John Treharne is a former accountant and England squash player whose experience in the fitness industry spans 29 years. In 1991 John started his first gym business, Dragons Health Clubs, which listed on the London Stock Exchange in 1997, with 22 clubs. Dragons was sold in 2000. He, then, lent his expertise to premium gym chain Esporta, before he concentrated on the launch of The Gym Group in 2008. Under John's leadership, The Gym Group pioneered the low-cost gym model with contract less, 24/7 operation and online sign-up. In November 2015, The Gym Group became the first UK health and fitness group to debut on the London Stock Exchange in over 15 years. In February 2016, the business was named as a finalist and Ruban d'Honneur recipient in the 2015/16 European Business awards. Today, The Gym Group is nationwide with 129 gyms and has a roll-out programme of 15-20 new gyms each year. It has had 100 million gym visits since its launch in 2008, and a membership of over 600,000.

From your perspective, what are the key factors that influence the demand for Personal Training today and in future?

We believe Personal Training is and will continue to be in increasing demand by the market. The main drivers for health club membership are people trying to achieve goals including weight loss, getting fit, or preparing for a marathon. Whatever they want to join a gym or health club for, they are looking for tangible results and Personal Training undoubtedly helps them achieve their goals. So, we see increasing future demand and it is slightly ironic that from the information we derive from our joining process the potential demand for Personal Training is at least double what the normal market experiences. And the reason for that is that about 36% of our members are first time gym users. They are interested in having Personal Training because they want to have programmes written and somebody to assist them in achieving their goals.

An additional factor we also see is the increasing number of people coming from UK universities with relevant qualifications, so sport hons degrees. I can remember when I first got involved in the health club business in the early 90s, it was only one or two universities that had training related degree courses. Today every university does. Therefore, there is an increasing number of bright young people entering the health and fitness industry from universities with suitable qualifications with many attracted by Personal Training; partly because of the income potential and partly for the flexibility that Personal Training affords.

Personal Trainers in our business, because they are self-employed, can charge whatever they like. The market demand leads them to about 30 pounds an hour depending on where in the country it is. In more affluent parts you can charge more. But that is where we believe the average level is. It's something that Personal Trainers have to consider. Should they charge a considerably more they can price themselves out of the market, because people cannot afford more per session. People are looking for Personal Training on a value for money basis.

How many Personal Trainers do you have? What are your process and metrics? And how does Personal Training work at The Gym Group?

Currently there are about 1,500 self-employed Personal Trainers working in our gyms across the country. The way these Personal Trainers work at the moment is very simple. There are about 10 to 12 Personal Trainers per gym. We offer them specific opportunities to market their Personal Training businesses to members (about 10 hours a week) and in that time, they will do things like inductions for new members, they show potential new members around our gyms which is giving them interaction with their potential customer base. And then, they can do as much Personal Training as they wish and they may keep all the revenue. The Gym Group makes absolutely nothing out of Personal Training, it is not a profit stream for us. It is a service we are enabling personal trainers to provide for our customers because we recognise that it enhances the customer experience. That is how it operates at the moment.

But we are looking at changing it. Because these Personal Trainers are genuinely self-employed we don't have as much control over what they do as we would like. For example, I can't enhance their skill set, but I want to be able to do that because it'll provide the best service to our customers. Consequently, we are introducing three new types of Personal Trainer roles. The one that we think will be most popular with the majority of our Personal Trainers is that they will work about 10 to 12 hours for us and we will pay them national minimum wage for those 10-12 hours.

Because we are paying them and because they will be employed for those parttime hours they are working for us, we will be able to train them and insist in our time that they do training and development of their skill set. The rest of the time they will be just self-employed and operate as they do currently. We see that process being cost neutral because we would be paying them the minimum wage for the hours they work for us. and in return for access to typically up to 6,000 members per club they would pay us a small rental that effectively covers those costs. We see that as being most of Personal Trainers.

In the second category the Personal Trainer just pays rent. They keep 100 % of their revenues. That will probably be the more experienced Personal Trainer who already has their own client base.

They already have a successful business and actually don't want to give up free hours.

In the third category is probably likely to be someone who has just left university who we would actually employ as an instructor. They would then progress into becoming a Personal Trainer in one of the other two categories. But the cost of employing them would be effectively covered by the rental that the person who doesn't want to give us free time would give us. So, we see the whole situation being cost neutral. with the big benefit being that we would have some control over when people are working in our gyms what they do and how they do it and have the ability to train them to be better at this.

What are the selection criteria you use in choosing the right people to work as a Personal Trainer in your company? Could you rate specific characteristics or experiences in their meaning?

The first thing that we obviously look for is they need to be suitably qualified. There is a national accreditation called REPs, the register of exercise professionals. There are four different levels of qualification. So, to be Personal Trainer you need to have at least a red level 3 qualification. That is a minimum requirement for us as those trainers can be suitably insured. If you don't have that you can't be a Personal Trainer with us. Level 4 is slightly higher and tends to cover more specialist areas where somebody has done additional training in a particular area for instance women exercising after pregnancy. So, that's the minimum requirement and a sports hons degree course gives you that level of qualification. It doesn't have to be a degree-based solution, there are a number of training schools where this qualification can be achieved. We won't allow anybody that doesn't have that qualification to deliver Personal Training in our gyms.

Thereafter, the main criteria for me is the individual being personable, outgoing, friendly, being a good people person. We actually use psychometric testing to help us understand personality traits. We are just as interested in the "EQ" of a candidate as the "IQ". If candidates are not good in working with people, they are not likely to be successful. So, that actually is the other biggest recruitment element we look at.

We have quite a few self-employed Personal Trainers who start working in our gyms on that basis. And then, after a period of time, they then apply to become an assistant manager. We have our own internal training programme and about 44% of our managers have joined our management training program. We then train them ourselves, but they have to have a fitness qualification at the start of the process.

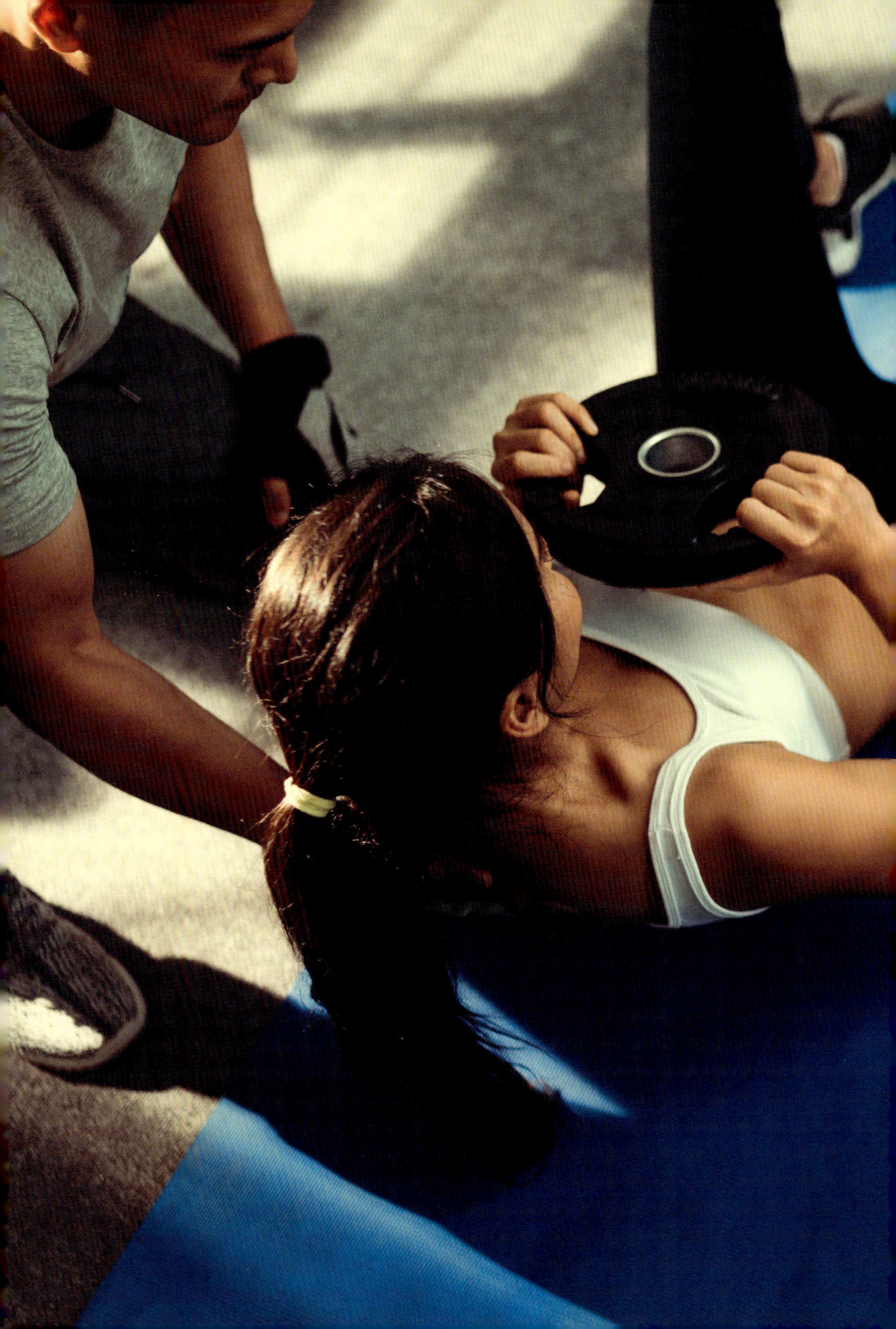

5 Method

5. Method

This study was executed using an online questionnaire that was setup to cover a wide range of questions. The survey was sent out in local (national) languages. Participants were fitness professionals and especially Personal Trainers. We recruited survey participants via different channels: EuropeActive contacted the members of their European Register of Exercise Professionals. In addition, we made use of multipliers by addressing relevant players in the individual national markets such as associations, education providers or club operators. Third, we searched the internet, Personal Trainer networks, and social networking services for direct contacts of individual Personal Trainers.

Our efforts resulted in a total of 4,370 fitness professionals who participated in the online survey that has been online from June to September 2017. 3,944 of them are located in the focused 15 European markets, and 2,819 of these are Personal Trainers. By far the strongest participation in total numbers was achieved in Italy where 500 Personal Trainers took part in our survey. Second-ranked is the United Kingdom with 352 participating Personal Trainers. Even in Switzerland, the country with the lowest absolute number of participating Personal Trainers, it is still as high as 98.

This study is of an exploratory nature. Thus, we are confident that the achieved participation numbers are a sound basis for our endeavour to get a first understanding of the Personal Training segment. Our data will reveal a detailed picture of the situation of Personal Trainers in the analysed countries. We will cover topics from Personal Trainers' characteristics to details of their operations or issues related to their clients to aspects concerning the overall market. Our survey data, however, will not be suitable to clarify market proportions and these participation numbers should not be confused with the actual market sizes.

General market data for the fitness sector is easily at hand, for example, in EuropeActive's Deloitte Market reports. When is comes to Personal Training, however, even basic information is lacking: There is little knowledge in the individual markets even with regard to the basic question of how many Personal Trainers there are currently offering their services. A major reason for this situation is that neither the term "Personal Training" is strictly defined nor "Personal Trainer" is a protected title. Hence, anyone offering for instance any kind of one-on-one training could call him- or herself a Personal Trainer in many countries. There is also a lack of clear organisation of Personal Training in some markets; some countries have a multitude of Personal Training associations, others have none.

To get at least an initial picture of the market size of Personal Training in different countries we have applied the numbers of the business- and employment-oriented social networking service LinkedIn. As of 31/12/2017 a total of 44,106 people stated that they are a Personal Trainer in their current job title. This attempt to approximate the respective market numbers obviously has its shortcomings. Obviously not every Personal Trainer is present in this specific network and its penetration, i.e. the portion of LinkedIn members in the total population, differs between the individual countries. Moreover, the title "Personal Trainer" seems to have different levels of awareness and importance in the various relevant languages. For instance, in French the "coach sportif", in Spanish the "entrenador personal", or in Dutch the "persoonlijke trainer" are also used.

Another indication that the actual number of Personal Trainers might be even higher than the 44,106 in the 15 countries is the growth we have determined from 30/06/2017 until the end of the year. Coming from 42,000 LinkedIn members who stated to have the job title "Personal Trainer" as of the end of June, the growth rate until 31/12/2017 is almost 5%. As the social networking service has been able to enlarge its overall member base in Europe in the same time span, the increase of Personal Trainers seems to be predominately driven by the growing market penetration of LinkedIn in Europe. Therefore, and again, our approach should be recognised as exploratory. Nevertheless, we believe it is worthwhile as a starting point and call for additional research on this fundamental question of market sizes.

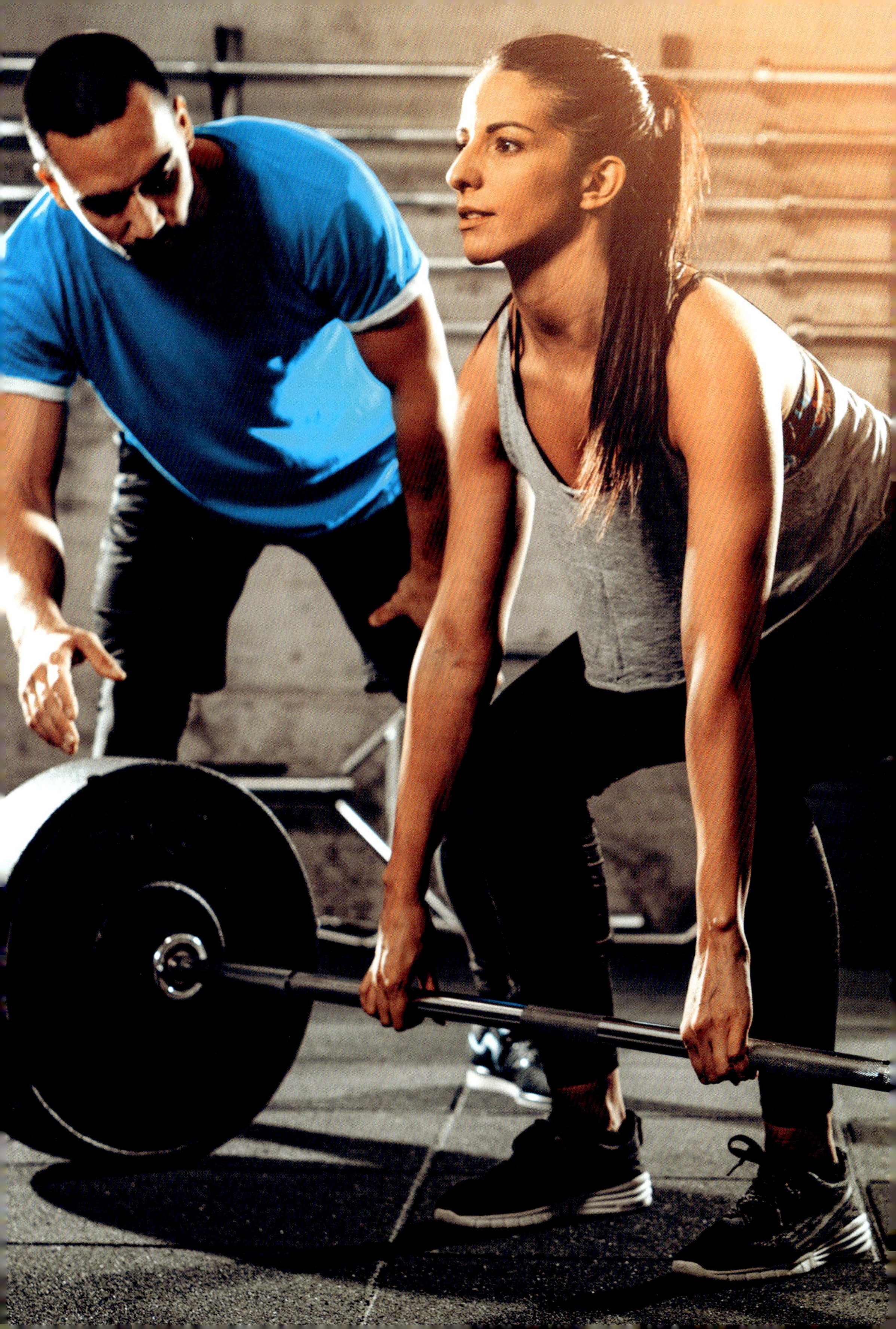

About EuropeActive, edelhelfer, Start2Move and BlackBoxPublishers

EuropeActive

EuropeActive is the leading not-for-profit organisation representing the whole of the European health and fitness sector in Brussels (www.europeactive.eu). The European health and fitness sector serves over almost 60 million consumers, generates over 27 billion Euro in revenues, employs an estimated 650,000 people, and consists of more than 53,000 facilities. Alongside its significant economic contribution, the sector has a major role to play in making a more active and healthy Europe. EuropeActive aims to co-operate with the European Union and other international organisations to achieve its objective to get:

MORE PEOPLE | MORE ACTIVE | MORE OFTEN

EuropeActive is also a standard setting body of the health and fitness sector and promotes best practice in instruction and training, with the ultimate objective to raise the quality of service and the customer's exercise experience and results. EuropeActive currently represents approx. 25,000 facilities with 21 national associations and a membership spread across 25 countries in Europe. Membership is open to all stakeholders – public or private – including operators, suppliers, national associations, training providers, and higher education and accreditation institutions.

EuropeActive fully supports the strategic principles and objectives of the EU Lifelong Learning Programme and its mission is to motivate people to embrace a lifelong active and healthy lifestyle. EuropeActive aims to achieve its vision by:

- Building and expanding awareness of the health benefits of regular physical activity and the cost and consequences of inactivity.
- Supporting networking and facilitating partnerships between the sector, academia, governments and civil society, in order to identify common challenges and opportunities.
- Contributing to the development of products and services that would ensure a favourable environment for each individual to develop skills, confidence and a healthy balance of body and mind.
- Ensuring that high quality standards are set in the fitness, physical activity and wellbeing sector, allowing users to enjoy safe and effective exercise.

Contact EuropeActive
Avenue des Arts 43
B-1040, Brussels, BRU
Belgium
Tel. +32 2 649 90 44
For more information about EuropeActive visit
http://www.europeactive.eu/

edelhelfer

edelhelfer

edelhelfer GmbH was named after the super-domestique in cycling (German: Edelhelfer). He works in an outstanding position for the success of his team captain and supports him in every situation of the race. While he also serves as a water carrier, he is particularly able to give his team captain slipstream in tough high mountain stages.

Following this analogy, we see ourselves as a partner accompanying our client on his specific way towards his aim. Thereby, the customer takes centre stage as the captain with whom we prepare each stage in the best possible way and also put the planning into practice. Our tasks can be as versatile as the challenges that arise in the different stages of business development. Market analysis, strategic positioning, or the acquisition of capital represent a major part of our work.

We mainly focus our services on the consumer goods industry and especially on the sports and leisure market where we already possess a broad "race history" which we can apply in our new tasks. The edelhelfer team works on individual and pragmatic solutions in a committed, flexible and also creative way for sustainable success in each stage of business development.

With the following range of services, we can support you at all stages of your corporate development:

Prologue · Conceptual design & foundation
- Start-up advice
- Market, competitive and location analysis
- Development and screening of business plans
- Support in the acquisition of equity and loan capital

Low mountain range · Strategic optimization
- Development of strategies
- Screening of service offers ("Mystery Shopping")
- (Re-)positioning analysis and advisory
- Organisational development

High mountain range · Expansion & growth
- Market and competitive analysis
- Development of expansion strategies
- Bank and investor communication
- Support in M&A activities

Contact edelhelfer

edelhelfer GmbH
Melchiorstraße 1–7
68167 Mannheim
Germany
Phone: +49 621 178857-27
Fax: +49 621 178857-19
Email: kontakt@edelhelfer.eu
http://www.edelhelfer.eu

Start2Move

In 2007, Jelmer Siemons established Start2Move in The Netherlands. Currently, Start2Move is the Dutch market leader in educations for fitness professionals. Most educations are recognized by the Government, with in total 25 locations and over 40 well-trained teachers.

The head office of Start2Move is located in Zwolle, were a dedicated team is working 24/7 to support fitness professionals. The company is structured by three academies: the fitness academy, the health academy and the sport academy, offering over 60 courses in total.

The core mission of Start2Move is to assist professionals in building their career, and support life-long learning. Start2Move is a partner of EuropeActive and has international ambitions. The Marketing and Support (CRM) System of Start2Move is of huge value to other training providers, and available within a license model.

Contact Start2Move
Hogeland 10
8024 AZ Zwolle
The Netherlands
Tel: 088 850 7648
Mail: info@start2move.nl
www.start2move.nl

BlackBoxPublishers

BlackBoxPublishers (BBP) is a publisher of books and e-books in the fitness, sport and health sector. BBP was founded in 2012 by Dr Johan Steenbergen (researcher), Peter van der Steege (designer and online marketing specialist), Dr Jan Middelkamp (researcher) and Kelby Jongen (consultant).

The mission of BlackBoxPublishers is to *facilitate fitness, health and sport professionals with world class content for growth.* See: www.blackboxpublishers.com. On top of this there is an open marketplace for fitness professionals: www.blackboxfitness.com.

BBP is the publishing partner of EuropeActive and has published books including The State of Research in the Global Fitness Industry (English, German and Dutch) (2012); Member Retention in Fitness Clubs (English, German and Dutch) (2013); The Future of Health & Fitness (2014); EuropeActive's Essentials of Motivation and Behaviour Change (English, Finnish and Dutch) (2015); Growing the Fitness Sector Through Innovation (2016); Customer Engagement and Experience in the Fitness Sector (English and Chinees) (2017); Human Capital (2018); and the EuropeActive Retention Reports 2013, 2014, 2015, 2016 and 2017.

Visit: www.blackboxpublishers.com

miha bodytec

DIVE INTO THE WORLD OF MIHA BODYTEC

A technology is striding ahead!

Electrical muscular stimulation – a ground-breaking way to train! The EMS market is growing dynamically and in a variety of manifestations: mobile personal trainers, special offers in existing facilities, and even dedicated EMS studios.

Active musculature is the key to a body with great capacity, as well as being a precondition for health, fitness, wellbeing, and an aesthetically pleasing appearance – in short, for that kind of physical and mental ability you've always really wanted. miha bodytec guarantees results that will astound you, results you can achieve rapidly, and results you can really see. Right in step with the spirit of our times!
- experience miha bodytec for yourself!

Headquarter • Siemensstr. 1 • D-86368 Gersthofen • Tel.: +49 821 45 54 92 - 0 • Fax: +49 821 45 54 92 - 29 • E-Mail: info@miha-bodytec.de
miha bodytec ems UK Ltd • UK Branch Office • 14 Gower's Walk • London E1 8PY United Kingdom • Office: +44 208 068078 0 • E-Mail: uk.info@miha-bodytec.com